Proserpina: Goethe's Melodrama with Music by Carl Eberwein

Proserpina: Goethe's Melodrama

with Music by Carl Eberwein

Orchestral Score, Piano Reduction, and Translation

edited by Lorraine Byrne Bodley

Carysfort Press

A Carysfort Press Book in association with Peter Lang

Proserpina: Goethe's Melodrama with Music by Carl Eberwein
Edited and translated by Lorraine Byrne Bodley

First published in Ireland in 2007 by Carysfort Press Ltd
58 Woodfield, Scholarstown Road, Dublin 16, Ireland

ISBN 978-1-78997-093-7

Enquiries about orchestral parts should be addressed to
lorraine.byrnebodley@nuim.ie
or to Carysfort Press

Typeset by Carysfort Press

Cover design by Brian O'Connor

This book is published with the financial assistance of
The Arts Council (An Chomhairle Ealaíon), Dublin, Ireland

For Margaret, beloved mother and friend

Contents

Acknowledgements

The idea for this score emerged through my writing the first English translation of the discussion of music in Goethe's letters to the composer, Zelter: *Goethe and Zelter: Musical Dialogues* (Ashgate, 2008). The volume of letters is a mine of information about musical life in Germany at that time (1797-1832) and contains many references to unfamiliar works by unknown composers, long omitted from the canon of musical works discussed and performed today. While working on this critical translation of Goethe's letters I familiarized myself with any music discussed in these letters which I did not already know. Searching through Goethe's private music collection in the Goethe and Schiller Archive in Weimar, I discovered the work of Carl Eberwein, an unknown composer, whose dramatic setting of Goethe's melodrama, *Proserpina*, is for solo voice (speaking part) and orchestra, with a choral finale. Struck by the highly dramatic impact of a manuscript which is beautifully orchestrated and notated, I immediately applied for a copy of the score, and showed it to my husband, Seóirse Bodley, who confirmed my immediate impression of the work. Excited by the discovery, I sent a copy of the score to the principal conductor of the RTE Symphony Orchestra, Gerhard Markson, who was immediately interested in performing it. We discussed the project with Brian O'Rourke, Orchestral Manager of National Symphony Orchestra, and the Irish premiere of this work was scheduled for Friday, 30 November 2007 in the National Concert Hall in Dublin, performed by the National Symphony Orchestra, the RTE Philharmonic choir, conducted by Gerhard Markson, with the German singer-actress, Elfi Hoppe in the role of Proserpina. I am immensely grateful to Gerhard Markson for the immediate interest he showed in the score, an interest that was pivotal in bringing it to professional performance.

This score has been in preparation for the past year, and I have been helped by many people. From the time I began, my husband, Seóirse Bodley, was prodigal of his assistance, allowing me to tap his extensive knowledge of preparing an orchestral score for performance. He also kindly read the manuscript, score and piano reduction, and suggested many improvements. He has my heartfelt thanks. Dr Dan Farrelly of Carysfort Press graciously put at my disposal his years of experience as a Germanist and extraordinary knowledge of the Goethe period, and I owe much to his generosity and guidance. The manuscript has been read by Dan Farrelly, from whose criticisms I have greatly profited. Professor Nicholas Boyle took time from his busy life to read my work; he also agreed to write the preface and give a lecture in Maynooth on the afternoon of the performance. The interest he expressed in Goethe's monodrama *Proserpina* at the conference *Goethe: Musical Poet, Musical Catalyst* in Maynooth in April 2004 ignited my initial interest in the melodrama. I feel very privileged that he should travel to Ireland during term time to attend the first performance of this score.

In preparing this edition I owe much to the acumen of Michael Casey, music copyist for this score, who patiently deciphered Eberwein's music from our first, less than adequate, A4 photocopy of the score. For his good-humour, professionalism and generosity with his time I am immensely grateful. I am especially grateful to Frau Evelyn Liepsch and Frau Wagner at the Goethe and Schiller Archive in Weimar, who not only hunted down the original manuscript for me to work with, but offered to make me an A3 photocopy of the autograph, which proved invaluable. I am also indebted to the Goethe and Schiller Archive for the newly-taken photographs of the original score for this publication.

I am grateful to the National University of Ireland Maynooth, for facilitating my research. The National University of Ireland Publications Scheme made this score possible by awarding me a publication grant. Thanks are due to the President of the National University of Ireland, Maynooth, Professor John Hughes, for his support and interest in this publication and performance; to Dr Barra Boydell, who warmly welcomed my suggestion of a research seminar on *Proserpina* in Maynooth on the afternoon of the performance. My chief gratitude must go to my friends, colleagues, and students of the Departments of Music and German – especially Professor Gerard Gillen – for their unfailing encouragement and support, and to Professor Fiona Palmer for her financial and moral support. The German Ambassador, Herr Christian Pauls, and the Director of the Goethe Institute, Herr Rolf Stehle, also have my warm thanks for their financial support of this research project.

I am grateful for the generous encouragement I have received from the Society of Musicology in Ireland: from the President of that Society, Professor Jan Smaczny (Hamilton Harty Professor of Music, Queen's University Belfast) who immediately agreed to give a guest lecture at the symposium and to support the project. My thanks are due to the inaugural President of the Society, Professor Harry White (Professor of Music, University College Dublin), who, with his usual generosity, agreed to launch this publication.

I have many specific acts of kindness to record from the following: Marie Breen and Dr Paddy Devine (Department of Music, NUIM); Minister Councillor, Clarissa Duvigneau (German Embassy, Dublin); Rolf Stehle and Barbara Ebert (Goethe Institute, Dublin); Cressida Kocienski (Tate Gallery, London); Professor Florian Krobb (Department of German, NUIM); Dr Michael Murphy (Honorary Secretary SMI), and Tina Talukder (Cultural Department, Embassy of the Federal Republic of Germany).

It is a privilege for me to thank everyone at Carysfort Press, first and foremost, Dr Dan Farrelly. I am profoundly grateful for my association – now relatively long – with this excellent press.

Finally, heartfelt thanks to my dear mother Margaret, to whom this book is dedicated: I will always be grateful for her time, her immense love, and her faith in me.

Lorraine Byrne Bodley

Editorial Note

This score is edited from the Manuscript Score *Proserpina: Monodrama von Goethe mit Musik von Carl Eberwein* (GSA 32 161) held in the *Goethe- und Schiller-Archiv*, Weimar. While my aim was to reproduce a score which follows Goethe's and Eberwein's artistic intentions faithfully, a number of editorial decisions were taken in order to present the score according to the standards of modern performance.

With regard to the orchestral score I have scored everything in concert pitch, as is common in many modern performance scores. (In the parts, the relevant instruments are scored as transposing instruments.) I have also altered Eberwein's trumpets in B flat and E flat to trumpets in C; his horns in G are now scored as Horns in F, and the top trombone part, originally written for alto trombone (now obsolete), becomes the first trombone part.

With regard to notation: in the original manuscript Eberwein frequently reiterates accidentals which are already in the key signature; occasionally he forgets accidentals (for example, the E natural on the second quaver beat of bar 158). Both have been corrected. This aside, it must be noted here that the autograph manuscript is, in fact, beautifully scored, in a clear hand and remarkably it contains very few notational errors.

The most important editorial remarks concern the music declamation. In melodrama, the declaimed text is rarely laid out rigorously against the music; performers take charge of the inflection and especially of the placement of their speech against the musical background, which can radically alter the meaning of the work. In the publication of his piano melodrama, *Leonore*, Liszt addresses this idea in his comment: 'The bars that are marked ||: : || may be repeated several times, according to necessity, in order to bring the music into agreement with the declamation.' In those passages where words are recited against the music, I have followed the practice of writing the words above each bar, though not necessarily in a syllable-to-note relationship. In the short antiphonal passages, where Proserpina and the orchestra alternate, I have frequently used the term *quasi recitativo*, which helps to clarify the style of the relationship between the soloist and the orchestra. In long passages spoken by Proserpina, I have scored the protagonist's lines over a single bar scored with a pause to indicate that the surrounding music is consistently in tempo. In both passages, I have followed the artistic intentions faithfully – a practice which is not observed in Peter Gülke's fine recording of the score (MDG 335 0740-2), where passages are declaimed against orchestral accompaniment which were originally scored as antiphonal passages. A good example of this is found at lines 14 to 28 which, in Gülke's version, is declaimed against the orchestral passage at rehearsal mark B followed by a newly-composed bridge passage scored at bars 288-294; lines 36 and 38 enter at bars 305 and 307 instead of being declaimed as a quatrain at bar 308. Although Gülke's fine interpretation is musically convincing, and the sheer intensity of Salome Kammer's reading of Proserpina is astonishing, it approaches the style of melodrama written later in the nineteenth century, and overlooks the attention Goethe paid to the exact declamation of Proserpina's lines. Proserpina's sinister fate is sealed from the opening g-minor chords – a destiny reiterated by the Fates at the end, where they pay homage to Proserpina as their Queen, knowing it is a role she longs to relinquish. Eberwein subtly captures this dramatic irony in the deliberately simple chorus, whose mocking reverence needs to be realized in performance.

In producing a scholarly performance edition I aimed to maximize the performance possibilities of Goethe's and Eberwein's score. Today, performances of melodrama – even in Germany – are exceedingly rare. Even presentations of them with piano are forgotten, for that close interrelationship of actors and musicians – which sprang from the late romantic ideal of fusing the arts – itself represents a past and forgotten preference for integrating music with language and literature. Examples of this preference still occur in the joint recitals of actors and singers at which an actor recites the poems to be sung by a singer: the aim of the actor is to recite with a musical delivery and the singer, on the other hand, to some extent imitates theatrical declamation. Such collaboration of musicians and non-singing actors – individuals who are nowadays often unaccustomed to performing together – is central to the spirit of melodrama.

A central question in performing Proserpina is: how are the actor and musician to synchronize the spoken text with the orchestral score? That Corona Schröter gave the premiere performance of *Proserpina* suggests that Goethe wished to realize his artistic intentions by using a highly-trained singer-actress. Goethe's text was delivered in a kind of elevated speech about which Wagner was later to theorize – essentially a type of recitation which the ancient Greeks were said to have used in performing their plays. Goethe's ideas of naturalistic expression are found in the dramatic passages which are recited in relatively normal speech. In those passages where the voice is synchronized with music Goethe approaches what was later realized in Humperdinck's *Sprechnoten*, where the melody of the spoken verse follows the rhythm and inflection of intensified speech. Although the poet was precise in his declamation of the text, Goethe allows the performer more freedom than in Humperdinck's idea of *gebundenes Melodram* (bound melodrama, where the spoken text is recited in a precise rhythm to musical background (*Sprechnoten*)).[1] Where Goethe's text is written across the bars 333 to 345, for example, it is clear from the manuscript that Goethe expected the singer/actress to declaim the lines quite freely. Of central importance is that the significance of Proserpina's plight should come across and so to Goethe's words and Eberwein's music we now must add the interpretative power of the performer.

Lorraine Byrne Bodley

[1] A good example of this is found in his *Königskinder*.

Preface

Proserpina is the most purely and starkly tragic of all Goethe's dramatic writings. The date and occasion of its composition are not certainly known, but it was probably written between June and December 1777, in a period of exceptional emotional turbulence for Goethe after the death of his twenty-six year-old sister Cornelia on 8 June. In its setting by Siegmund von Seckendorff it had one independent performance by Weimar's recently acquired professional singer, Corona Schröter, in the theatre of the Dowager Duchess Anna Amalia at Ettersburg on 10 June 1779. It had however already been premiered by Corona Schröter as an insertion into the satirical farce *Der Triumph der Empfindsamkeit*, which was put on by the court amateurs on 30 January 1778, the birthday of Duchess Luise, the wife of the reigning Duke, and was repeated on 10 February of the same year. Goethe much later expressed regret at the incorporation of *Proserpina* into this alien context, an act of vandalism which, by making his deeply-felt monodrama the target of coarse mockery, had deprived it of all its effect. Why should he have felt compelled to mutilate his own creation? Evidently he realized that he had exposed to public view something especially personal and disquieting.

In the monodrama, as in the myth on which it is based, Proserpina has been snatched out of a world of light and flowers and condemned to marriage to an unloved husband - like Cornelia, and like other taboo women who fascinated Goethe at the time, such as Frau von Stein and Duchess Luise. Alone in a desolate and mournful subterranean landscape Proserpina calls for aid to Jupiter, her loving father, as she thinks. A pomegranate tree seems sent to offer her refreshment and a sign of hope that her prayer has been heard, but when she eats the fruit she is seized by the terrible certainty that this act has cursed her and she can never now be released from her torment. The drama ends in despair, and with no hint of the consoling resolution offered by the myth – that Proserpina will at least be allowed by Jupiter to return to the upper world every six months.

Proserpina has been betrayed by her own notion of hope and trust in a loving divinity - as in Goethe's ode 'Prometheus' of 1773, God is either non-existent or malevolent. But Prometheus can boast of all that his 'sacred and burning' heart has achieved, by contrast with the silent and impotent god whom he scorns. Proserpina has nothing to point to that her heart has done for her. On the contrary, the shipwreck of her life seems to have been brought about precisely by a trust that her heart could not ultimately mislead her. Is then the love and beauty and perfection which is our heart's desire an illusion? The very act by which Proserpina expresses her faith that it is not an illusion, her eating the fruit that seems an answer to her prayer, condemns her. She is left to an eternity not merely of unfulfilment, but of punishment for allowing herself to hope she might be fulfilled. How reliable are our needs as a guide to the order of things outside ourselves? Are these yearnings an inexplicable and self-imposed torment? Or is the heart sufficient unto itself, requiring neither validation nor satisfaction of its needs from an external power? Goethe had been agitated by these questions since the crisis of the Sentimentalist movement that he had represented in his novel *Werther*, the story of a feeling heart that destroys itself. Like Werther, Proserpina in her deepest need puts her trust in her heart and is betrayed. By 1777 Goethe knew that in his own life he had to put behind him the possibility of such a tragedy of 'innocent guilt', or like Cornelia, and many other contemporaries less close to him, he would be eaten up by unproductive absorption in the inadequacy of the world to his emotions. Though he had given bitter and unsparing expression to Proserpina's fate, he had to shake off his sympathy with it in order to survive. Her tragedy was therefore incorporated into the brutal parody of Sentimentalism in *Der Triumph der Empfindsamkeit* and lost to view for a generation.

Early in 1814 Goethe's favourite actor, Pius Alexander Wolff, suggested to the local composer Carl Eberwein that he should write a new score for the forgotten monodrama, probably with a view to creating an opportunity for his wife Amalie, *née* Malcolmi. (It is possible that Goethe put the idea into Wolff's mind, but there is no evidence.) On Whitsunday 1814 Eberwein played his composition to Goethe on the piano, while Goethe's secretary Riemer declaimed the text and Goethe found himself deeply moved. At some later date Goethe and Eberwein went through the work privately together. A production was set in train at the end of the year, and the new *Proserpina* was first performed on 4 February 1815, to mark the birthday of Weimar's heir apparent, the thirty-two year-old Carl Friedrich, with Amalie Wolff, also thirty-two, in the title-role. The performance was such a success that it was repeated a further three times, and enquiries came in from other theatres interested in putting the work on themselves. For their benefit, Goethe published in Cotta's *Morgenblatt für gebildete Stände* on 8 June 1815 an account of his intentions, only partly realized in the Weimar production.

The stage set, which in Weimar had to be purely schematic, should, Goethe thought, show the underworld as a sombre Poussinesque landscape of ruined castles, aqueducts and bridges. All the achievements of civilization should be shown returning to a state of nature, since for the ancients – as Goethe had already argued in an essay on the wall-paintings of Delphi in 1804 – the worst punishments in the after-life were those that revealed the pointlessness of human activity. The ruin of a villa, with its garden now a wilderness, would also help explain the presence of the pomegranate tree. Proserpina should enter weighed down with the splendid robes, veils and diadem that signified her hateful condition as Pluto's queen, but should cast these off in order to emerge as the flower-crowned nymph who first roused the god's desire in the vale of Enna. One garment should be retained however which she could use to enhance her gestures in the manner of Emma Hamilton's 'attitudes' (poses, sometimes in a specially constructed picture frame, representing a character from literature or art), to which Goethe had been introduced when he visited Sir William Hamilton, the British ambassador in Naples, in 1787. (Goethe may also have known that Lady Hamilton had died in wretched circumstances only a month before this production.) Both the 'attitudes' and the *tableaux vivants* which developed out of them – the imitation by living but stationary actors of well-known paintings – had proved popular in Germany, and Goethe laid emphasis in his essay on the elaborate tableau with which the Weimar production concluded. During the final choruses the set opened to reveal Pluto on his throne, with the three Fates in a cave beneath him and beside him an empty throne awaiting Proserpina. To his left, Tantalus, Ixion, and Sisyphus were shown in semi-darkness suffering in solitude the pains of endless and fruitless exertion, while to his right the blessed were rewarded in light with the social joys of love and family life. (The graded illumination from left to right permitted the scene painter to include the full range of colours which in Goethe's theory are created by the mingling of light and darkness.) By contrast with the elaborate movements of the singer-dancer-actress the motionless tableau showed 'the kingdom of shades ... frozen into a picture, and the queen too freezing into a part of the image'. In a final *coup-de-théâtre* the curtain fell and after a few moments rose again during the last bars of the piece to show the same scene, but with Proserpina now enthroned and at last perfectly still, her gaze averted from the spouse to whom she is bound in eternity.

By 1815 Goethe had developed a new practice of tragedy, and was well on his way to developing a new theory of it. By concluding his monodrama with a Hamiltonian tableau he was able to achieve an aesthetic distancing which muted its emotional impact, and made it possible to enjoy a work the theme of which was an extremity of despair. He had already had recourse to similar tableaux at or near the end of other tragedies, such as *Egmont* and *Torquato Tasso*. By inserting *Proserpina* into *The Triumph of Sensibility* he had also sought to detach himself and his audience from the terrible implications of the story he had told, but he had now found a way of doing so without compromising the tragedy of Proserpina's end, and without destroying the deep seriousness of the play.

Goethe already intended his collaboration with Eberwein on *Proserpina* to issue in what the age of Wagner came to know as a *Gesamtkunstwerk*, a work of all the arts. All friends of Goethe can be grateful to Dr Lorraine Byrne Bodley for recovering and making available this profound little masterpiece. Let us hope that theatres around the world will now discover in it a means of giving their audiences the pleasures of a *Gesamtkunstwerk* without requiring them to sit still in Bayreuth for fifteen hours.

Nicholas Boyle

Proserpina
Goethe's Melodrama with Music by Carl Eberwein

Lorraine Byrne Bodley

Imagining Proserpina

For more than twenty-five centuries, the Proserpina myth[1] has occupied a central position in both the collective unconscious and the collective consciousness of people in Western cultures[2] and has invited widely different interpretations.[3] The explosive energy of Bernini's *The Rape of Proserpina*, which portrays Proserpina's pathetic attempt to defend herself against Pluto,[4] directly contrasts with the sensuality of Rembrandt's *The Abduction of Proserpina* (1630).[5] Likewise the heroine of Monteverdi's opera, *Proserpina rapita*[6] is radically different from Jean-Baptiste Lully's *Proserpina*,[7] which plays on the popularity of mythological rapes in seventeenth-century France and allowed artists to test the limits of the representability of sexual desire. And as one would expect, Lorenzo da Ponte's treatment of the legend in the *Ratto di Proserpina*, set to music by Peter von Winter and performed in London in 1804,[8] represents a radically different sound world to Stravinsky's *Persephone* which interprets the cycles of Proserpina's legend.[9]

The equally compelling literary images of this mythic text brilliantly illuminate the personal and cultural codes of the writers from which they spring. Hundreds of literary images of Proserpina exist from Homer's classical-period ancient Greece to Cixous's postmodern France, from Chaucer's medieval England to Atwood's contemporary Canada, from Quinault's France under Louis XIV to Morrison's 1940s America, all of which contain feminist or cultural criticism. While the myth of Proserpina originated from a rich oral tradition, the anonymous, fragmentary Homeric 'Hymn to Demeter',[10] is, in fact, the earliest source we have for the story of Proserpina and is the first full transcription of this mythological tale.[11] There is strong evidence that Ovid was familiar with the Homeric 'Hymn to Demeter'[12] and used it as a source for his version of the Proserpina story in his *Metamorphosis*, whose popularity and availability over the past two millennia has done much to spread the Proserpina myth to Western cultures. Many writers including Chaucer, Quinault, and Hawthorne, have taken their Proserpinas from Ovid and his successors. Another source for many modern writers, is Milton, who weaves the Proserpina myth, as told by Ovid in his *Metamorphoses*, into *Paradise Lost*, Book Four, as a trope for rape and links Pluto's ravishment of Proserpina with the seduction of Eve.[13] It is surprising how many poets have taken into their account this story of Proserpina to frame their own literary versions. From Shelley to Swinburne; from Rossetti to Meredith; from Tennyson to Heine; from Oscar Wilde to D.H. Lawrence; from Robert Bridges to Eavan Boland:[14] all of these writers have created their own images of Proserpina, maintaining her myth in the modern world. Their re-telling of the Proserpina story always involves some changes, variations to a theme that the author chooses on the basis of circumstances or his or her personal preferences. Part of the vitality of these readings is the way the myth constantly becomes charged with new meanings and absorbs new interpretations that open it up to new dimensions of reality yet to be discovered or re-explored'.[15] Walter Pater defined such classical and modern literary records of a myth as the 'poetical phase'.[16] In his analysis of the Greek myth of Ceres and Proserpina, Pater defines three stages: the first phase as the unwritten legend, passed on by oral tradition; the second phase as the poetical; the third phase as the ethical one, 'in which the persons and the incidents of the poetical narrative are realized as abstract symbols, intensely characteristic examples of moral or spiritual conditions.' So what do we know about Goethe's analogue to the Proserpina story? When was it written? What ethics inspired it? Why was Goethe preoccupied with this myth over a period of thirty-seven years? Ultimately, what is the modern meaning of Proserpina's mythical tale?

The Myth of Proserpina: Goddess, Maiden and Queen

Proserpina is an ancient maiden goddess whose story is the basis of a myth of Springtime. Her name comes from *proserpere* meaning 'to emerge', meaning the growth of the grain in Spring. Her Greek name, 'Persephone', is also derived from the Greek meaning 'splendidly lit.' She is a life-death-rebirth deity.

In Classical mythography, Proserpina was the daughter of Ceres (Demeter) and Jupiter (Jove), and was described as a very enchanting young girl. In order to bring love to Pluto, Venus sent her son, Amor, to hit Pluto with one of his arrows. Meanwhile Proserpina was in Sicily, at the fountain of Alpheus, in the vale of Enna,[17] where she was playing with the two nymphs, Cyane and Arethusa,[18] who were attendant upon her. In this setting of bucolic innocence, Proserpina was gathering flowers by the stream of Alpheus[19] when Pluto came out from the volcano Etna with four black horses and abducted the goddess in order to marry and live with her in

Hades, the dark Greek Underworld of which he was the ruler.[20] In terror, she dropped some of the lilies she had been gathering, [21] and they turned to daffodils:

> O Proserpina!
> For the flowers now that frighted thou let'st fall
> From Dis's waggon! daffodils,
> That come before the swallow dares, and take
> The winds of March with beauty...

Shakespeare, *The Winter's Tale*, IV, 3

After Proserpina was transported to the realm of Pluto, Proserpina's mother, Ceres, the goddess of the Earth, went in search of her daughter in every corner of the earth. For nine days and nights she wandered the earth without sleep in torment and despair, carrying torches to light her path in her nocturnal search; but it was unavailing. All she found was a small sash belonging to her daughter floating in the fountain of Cyane, an eponymous pool formed from the nymphs' tears of lamentation. In her despair, Ceres angrily scorched the earth, placing a malediction on Sicily. Recognizing Jupiter as an accomplice to Pluto's crime, Ceres refused to return to Mount Olympus and recommenced her pilgrimage, forming a desert with every step. Worried, Jupiter sent to his brother, Pluto, the messenger, Mercury, with an order to release Proserpina. Pluto acquiesced but the Fates would not allow Proserpina to be fully released; before letting her go, Pluto made her eat six pomegranate seeds (a symbol of fidelity in marriage) so she would have to live six months of every year with him, and enjoy the remaining months with her mother, Ceres.[22]

Pluto's decree grants us the reason for Springtime: when Proserpina returns to her mother, Ceres decorates the earth with welcoming flowers, but when in the Autumn Ceres changes the leaves to brown and orange (her favourite colours) as a gift to Proserpina before she returns to Hades, nature loses all its vibrant colour.

Proserpina's Odyssey: Modern Meaning of this Mythical Tale

The abduction of Proserpina from Arcadia is an intensely moving story, which has not lost its actuality today. Its emotionally charged narrative represents the marriage of a maiden and her separation from her mother as an experience so frightening she imagines she is dying. The mother, in turn, experiences the absence of her daughter as final and mourns her as if she had lost her forever. Even though the story is told almost always from the point of view of the feminine protagonist, it represents the coming of age of a young person so poignantly that people of all ages can relate to it. Children find their worst nightmare come to life – forced separation from their mother at the hands of an abductor; adolescents of both genders can ponder the experience of initiation that they themselves may be going through or may anticipate as forthcoming; adults find in the myth a representation of their own experiences of tragic loss and grief. Both men and women alike find in the myth a compelling evocation of the archetypal mother; a 'loving and terrible' mother. Essentially the story represents the loss that awaits both children and their parents: the loss of childhood innocence and the parents' loss of a child to time.

The Art of Retelling: Goethe's *Proserpina* (1778)

The reasons for Goethe's preoccupation with the myth of *Proserpina* have been subject to debate. Bode identifies *Proserpina* as the poem which Goethe wanted to write – on Wieland's mediation – to mark the death of Gluck's beloved niece, Nanette. Boyle with his keen critical insight places the melodrama as a lamentation for the early death of Goethe's sister, Cornelia on 8 June 1777.[23] Another reading is that Goethe wanted to write a star role for Corona Schröter,[24] who first performed the monodrama for the Duchess Luise's birthday on 31 January 1778,[25] in the ducal theatre of Weimar. The first independent publication of this prose-version of Goethe's text was arranged in conjunction with this premiere on 28 January 1778 and a separate publication appeared in Wieland's *Teutscher Merkur* in the first issue of 1778.

The following year a revised version of *Proserpina* in verse form was inserted into Act Four of Goethe's satirical drama *Der Triumph der Empfindsamkeit* (1778/79), a play within a play, performed by a highly-wrought queen, introduced by a rhymed prologue of Askalaphus, alias court servant. In this context the ironic handling of the abduction of Proserpina and the accompanying image of a lost paradise is presented as an example to the courtly women. Goethe's first reference to this version is in a letter to Charlotte von Stein on 12 September 1777,[26] where he announces *Der Triumph der Empfindsamkeit* as a comic opera: *Die Empfindsamen*. Goethe performed this play in Ettersburg in 1779, together with the actress, Corona Schröter, whose extraordinary abilities as actress and singer, inspired Baron Carl Siegmund von Seckendorff's setting of the same year. Seckendorff's handling of Proserpina's monologue differed from the strict form of contemporary melodramas, in which purely declaimed passages alternated with orchestral passages, in that it contained passages of melodramatic treatment along with arioso songs. Goethe also intensified the dramatic component of the text through the exchange between Proserpina and the Fates, which follows the principle of Gluck's classical choral opera, making this early work a hybrid mixture of musical forms. Bode's recognition of *Der Triumph der Empfindsamkeit* as 'a festival piece with songs and dances'[27] acknowledges the musical context of this early work, which is rooted in the tradition of the satirical Shrovetide play – comparable to the *Jahrmarktsfest zu Plundersweilern* – and belongs to the lively *Empfindsamkeitsparodien* of the Weimar court. Although Goethe published this poetic version in volume four of the

Schriften of 1787, in the early 1820s he regretted this 'dramatic whim' in the *Tag und Jahresheften* because, 'criminally placed in the *Triumph der Empfindsamkeit* [...] its effect was [then] destroyed'.[28]

In 1815, Goethe decided to create a more complete work that joined word, music and theatre; he revised the work as a melodrama, with music by Carl Eberwein, creating a very emotional piece, concentrating on the sorrow of the character. As a melodrama, its plot is very restricted, yet the condensed dramatic action intensifies its message. Musically and artistically, Goethe was very much involved in the composition of this work.[29] As is characteristic of his music-theatrical works, Goethe treated the work as a *Gesamtkunstwerk*, paying much attention to every aspect of it, especially to its music and its *mise en scène*, for which he took inspiration from Poussin's paintings.

Goethe's *Proserpina* and the Disappearing Eden

Although he took inspiration from Ovid's *Metamorphoses,* Goethe's analogue to the Proserpina story does more than pay tribute to his Greek and Roman predecessors or universalize the experience of the tale. Equally important from an aesthetic point of view is the way in which Goethe's monodrama strays from the usual mythical and melodramatic patterns to re-emerge as a fascinating blend of the 'realistic' and the 'archetypal'. In the ancient myth as well as in some of the modern versions, one finds examples of conciliation and compromise where deeply-felt loss is turned to gain: the father yields to the distraught mother; Ceres is prepared to share her daughter with her son-in-law; her anger subsides as death is conquered in what may be termed the resurrection of Proserpina; Ceres restores to the world the nourishment she had withdrawn; the cycle of the seasons offers a promise of renewal after deprivation and happiness after grief. Goethe's *Proserpina* offers no such solace. Whereas the ancient myth characteristically begins its seasonal cycle in the spring, Goethe's text opens in winter: a sign that this text will turn expectations upside down. The melodrama opens with Proserpina already in the underworld, relating her tragic experience of abduction. As Margherita Cottone has rightly observed in her article, 'Kore', Goethe underlines Proserpina's tragic condition of being Pluto's wife, queen of the underworld.[30] There is no reference to her return to the world and this makes more sorrowful her state of solitude. She meets the sad figures of the underworld – Tantalus, Ixion – and helpless, she can do nothing for them. She is doomed to be queen of the underworld forever and her evocative recollections of the past are a poignant reminder of the world she has left behind.

Parallels and Paradoxes in Goethe's *Proserpina*

Standing on a seasonal threshold, Proserpina's traditional symbolism renders her an ambiguous figure; she is a Janus-faced goddess depending on which one of the contrasted aspects of her nature is seized. Walter Pater defined her as 'the last day of spring or the first day of autumn'.[31] A virgin who gathers flowers in an uncorrupted place becomes queen of the underworld – connected with death and mystery – and goddess of rebirth, a liminal figure who occupies both the world of the dead and the living. Proserpina is thus a paradoxical figure in mythology embodying a dynamic tension between sun and shadow; she represents a contiguous positioning of opposite but equal qualities: temporal changes versus permanence; wilderness versus civilization; consciousness and unconsciousness; rationality and non-rationality.

Goethe's depiction of *Proserpina* maintains the obvious paradoxes common to this myth. His monodrama is anachronistic; it presents contemporary experience in an ancient myth which captures the duality of the heroine in its language (ll.156-59):

Daß mir Phöbus wieder Seine lieben Strahlen bringe, Luna wieder Aus den Silberlocken lächle!	That Phoebus may bring me His lovely rays once more, That Luna may Smile at me again from her silvery tresses!

Proserpina's face is lit by moonbeams which will chase all shadows of the underworld away.[32] She savours the fruits which makes her return impossible (ll.229-30):

Warum sind Früchte schön, Wenn sie verdammen?	Why are fruits so beautiful If they bring damnation?

Goethe captures this duality in the contrast between sequences: one moment Proserpina is an innocent child gathering flowers in an idyllic landscape (ll.14-28); a stark contrast to the hellish imagery of the next in which she suffers violence and a loss of innocence (ll.29-40). Perhaps out of such innocence, Proserpina is able to temper her grief with hope so that she is able to bear the experience (ll.160-178); one minute she unknowingly eats the pomegranate seeds (ll.179-197), in the next the 'fruit of paradise' seals her reign in hell (ll.179-216). The three grey-headed goddesses answer in one voice that Proserpina's fate was decided by a Fate beyond their own (ll.217-221):

DIE PARZEN (*unsichtbar*): Du bist unser! Ist der Ratschluß deines Ahnherrn:	**THE FATES** (*invisible*): You are ours! Your ancestor has so ordained!
Nüchtern solltest wiederkehren; Und der Biß des Apfels macht dich unser!	You were to return, sober, And the bite of the pomegranate makes you ours.

Such paradoxes highlight an important characteristic of Proserpina as the goddess of cycles and the cyclical patterns of Goethe's monodrama pivot on the passage of time: Proserpina describes her fate (ll.1-13) and then turns to the nymphs (ll.14–35); she recalls her abduction by Pluto, whose mask of death mirrors the moribund imagery around her (ll.36-100); she addresses her mother (ll.101-105); she recalls her mother roaming the Earth seeking her with the lamenting nymphs (ll.106-17) and then traces her mother's steps as she searches for her still (ll.118-40); it is interesting that Proserpina herself should address Jupiter (ll.141-69) and then turn to her surroundings, the Elysian fields, with hope (ll.170-79) before finding and eating the pomegranate seeds (ll.180-97) which seal her fate (ll.198 to the end).

The cycles of Goethe's monodrama are thus invoked by the metaphor of Proserpina. By opening the story with an interior monologue, Goethe immediately draws the reader into the protagonist's point of view; he reveals her true predicament at the beginning and augurs the final outcome through subtle changes wrought in the protagonist's status. The monodrama opens in Proserpina's grim underground garden, the 'fields of sorrow' where nothing grows. The allegory of Proserpina's garden and the moribund imagery of death hold no glimmer of hope: 'And what you seek *forever* lies behind you', Proserpina admits in the first quatrain. Her eternal fate is again augured by Arethusa's silence about the whereabouts of Proserpina when questioned by her distraught mother, Ceres.[33] Proserpina's monologue is framed by her recognition of the finality of death, again evident in the long dialogue with the Fates towards the end. The Fates address Proserpina five times, each time reinforcing her new identity as Queen of Hades. Their choral finale is reiterative – repeating exactly what Proserpina does not wish to see – yet they insist on such repetitions, unchanging patterns, transformations gone awry. By placing Proserpina at the beginning of the monodrama but letting the Fates have the final word, Goethe marks the transition in Proserpina's fate. Her marriage to Hades is the figurative death of innocence, a death in life. So instead of becoming a symbol of renewed fertility after a descent to the underworld (*catabasis*), Proserpina inhabits a waste land, barren, isolated and sterile.

Death and the maiden: Proserpina's initiation into adulthood

Departing from Ovid's *Metamorphoses*, Goethe conforms to the courtly conventions of dramatic *bienséances* by playing down the sexual aspect of the rape. Clearly, the euphemization of rape under the name of abduction would have pleased the sensibilities of the Weimar court in 1778/79. In Goethe's monodrama the rape of Proserpina is not sexually explicit: the violence of her abduction stands in for the sexual. Yet the pace of Goethe's lines gives the feeling that rape cannot be undone, that it will be carried to its end, no matter what forces attempt to counteract it. In Ovid, the rape causes the victim's mother to revolt against a social order that conceals her daughter's disappearance beneath a veil of silence. In Goethe's monodrama Ceres' silence can be explained by conventions of verisimilitude within the world of music theatre. Yet the underlying reason for Ceres' silence is that such marriages were sanctioned by society – a motif familiar to the court where marriages were arranged. Goethe questions this as he did in *Erwin und Elmire*, and his poetic version of Proserpina's ravishment is a complex entity, subversive to society.

Although Goethe picks up on Ovid's introduction of Cupid into the myth (ll.40-44):

Amor! ach Amor! floh lachend auf zum Olymp	Amor, O Amor! fled laughing up to Olympus!
Hast du nicht, Mutwilliger! Genug an Himmel und Erde? Mußt du die Flammen der Hölle Durch deine Flammen vermehren?	Have you not enough, you wanton, In heaven and on earth? Do you have to increase the flames of hell With your own flames?

Goethe's heroine is not tricked into tasting seeds of the dangerous fruit by Ascalaphus: it is an act of choice which condemns her to Hades. Although this episode can be given a classical sexual interpretation, Goethe's libretto explains Proserpina's action as an innocent attempt to quench her thirst. This sense of innocence permeates Goethe's text, where Proserpina's golden world is a pastoral paradise which mirrors the narcissism of its inhabitants. The false security of this pastoral idyll rests precariously on an unnatural commitment to stasis, on the elimination of seasonal and human metamorphosis. In Ovid's version of the tale, the false hope of perpetual spring is replaced by the fruitful round of the seasons, the sterile solipsism of the young by the metamorphosis of the self in marriage. For those pathologically intent on denying the fluidity of the self, Ovidian transformation is a kind of 'ritual death'.[34] Ovid's Proserpina is inclined to agree to the compromise of Jupiter for lack of a better choice: her initiation into adulthood is forced upon her, yet she is open to the personal metamorphosis that the admission of eros brings. Through this death-rebirth archetype, Ovid insists on the rightness of erotic life and the many changes it brings; he indicates the healthfulness of a more protean and thus a more fully human sense of self-identity. In Goethe's monodrama, *Proserpina*'s rejection of eros – first signalled by the notable absence of sexual imagery in Pluto's ravishment of Proserpina – leads to a forced and unfortunate metamorphosis and, in this respect, his heroine's protestation is more like Daphne's demand for *virginitas perpetua*. So why is Love's metamorphosis not enacted by Goethe?

Greek Goddesses, Human Lives

The answer to this question can be found in the date of the monodrama, 1777, the year of the death of Goethe's only sister, Cornelia.[35] In Goethe's monodrama the mythological and the confessional are brought together, and Goethe's whole story can be interpreted as Cornelia's coming of age, her initiation and passage into adulthood. Like her brother, Cornelia Goethe had received an exceptional education[36] and, unlike many women of her time, she had the privilege of choosing her husband. At the beginning she seemed delighted with her decision: '...all my hopes, all my wishes are not only fulfilled but surpassed by far. Let such a man be given to one whom God loves'[37] and everyone around her mirrored her happiness. Her father agreed to the considerable dowry of 10,000 fl. which remained under his control, but every year on their wedding anniversary he paid its interest of 400 fl. to his son-in-law. Cornelia's husband, Johann Georg Schlosser, was convinced of his good fortune in love and praised his wife as noble and tender:

> My beloved is now my wife! The loveliest female soul I could have wished for: noble, tender, upright! I needed such a woman in order to be happy.[38]

Even her brother admitted a positive development in her life. Only with the benefit of hindsight could Goethe state in his autobiography that his sister was talked into it. Here he describes Schlosser as a man with the best intentions, longing for moral perfection, whose serious, strict and possibly stubborn nature would have made him a social outsider, had he not possessed a rare literary education, knowledge of languages, and the much admired gift to express himself in verse and prose. And in conversation with Eckermann, just a year before he died, Goethe identified Cornelia's 'unfemale' character as the root of certain problems arising in her marriage:

> [...] she had very high moral standards with no trace of the sensual. The idea of giving herself to a man was repugnant to her, and one can only imagine that this peculiarity produced many an unpleasant hour in their marriage.[39]

Goethe's belief that his sister was absolutely devoid of sensuality is affirmed by Cornelia Goethe's husband. He complains in a letter to his brother that 'she finds my passion repulsive' and he mentions it again in his short allegory, *Ehestandsscene*, published in 1776, where he describes a state of alienation between husband and wife.[40] Schlosser pointed to Cornelia's unusual education as the fundamental reason for the difficulties in their marriage. Whatever the reason it is clear that in the early years of their marriage, love became a phantom for Cornelia, carrying with it the illusion that it is the solution for all problems. Yet when Cornelia realized that her ideas of gaining happiness and freedom as Schlosser's wife were mere illusions, her reaction seems to have been a complete withdrawal from reality. After the birth of their first child, she became increasingly melancholic. Various factors – individual and social – contributed to this melancholic despair expressed in her final letter to Countess Stolberg on 10 December 1776, where she paints a picture of her isolation in Emmendingen. In this letter, her desire to be just someone's sister once again echoes Proserpina's nostalgic yearning for the restoration of past certainties and comforting hierarchies:

> I sensed your domestic happiness and longed to be adopted as a sister by you; that is one of those wishes that will never be fulfilled, because our mutual distance is so great that I do not even dare to hope ever to see you in this life. We are completely isolated here. Not a single person is to be found within a 30-40 mile radius: my husband's business allows him to spend very little time with me, and so I crawl along slowly through the world, with a body which is fitting for nothing but the grave. I always find winter unpleasant and arduous; here nature's beauty is our only joy, and when it sleeps everything slumbers.[41]

Four weeks after the birth of her second daughter, at the age of 26, Cornelia died on 8 June 1777. Goethe's reaction to the loss was one of dark despair: 'Dark lacerated day',[42] he wrote in his diary. To his mother he confided: 'With my sister I have had so great a root struck off which bound me to the earth that the branches up above that had their nourishment from it must die also'.[43] And to Augusta Stolberg he wrote:

> The gods give everything
> to their favourites:
> Boundless joy,
> Infinite sorrow.[44]

Looking back on her life, Goethe confessed to Eckermann that he would never think of his sister as married – he would have rather imagined her as Abbess of some monastery. Goethe's image of his sister coincides with the portrait of Cornelia in Lenz's *Die Moralische Bekehrung eines Poeten, von ihm selbst aufgeschrieben*. For Lenz, Cornelia was a platonic lover and muse: 'angel of Heaven', 'idol of my head and heart', 'assuager and object of all my desires'.[45] While Lenz clearly portrayed Cornelia Goethe as an ideal woman woven into his literary world, it is interesting that his depiction should be mirrored in the epitaph Goethe writes for his sister in *Dichtung und Wahrheit*: 'she possessed everything which is expected of a person of such high condition; she lacked [everything] that the world demands as essential'.[46]

In *Dichtung und Wahrheit*, Goethe recorded his desire to erect an artistic memorial to his sister:

> I am not happy to be making a mere general statement about what I undertook to portray years ago but was unable to complete. When I lost this beloved, enigmatic person so prematurely, I felt I had every reason for bringing her merits to mind, and so I conceived the idea of a poetic whole which would make it possible to depict her individuality; but the only imaginable form for it was that of the novels of Richardson. Only by means of the most precise detail and infinite particulars which are all vividly characteristic of her whole self and which give some idea of this remarkable individual since they are wonderfully deep-rooted, would it have been to

> some extent possible to give an impression of this strange person; for a spring can only be imagined as flowing. But I was diverted from this fine, pious intention, as from so many others, by the tumult of the world; and now I have no alternative but to summon up the shade of that blessed spirit for just a moment, as though with the aid of a magic mirror.[47]

Although Goethe was unable to write this memorial to his sister, the personal drama suffered by Cornelia is voiced in *Proserpina*, where love consummates the heroine's isolation. Like Proserpina, Cornelia withdrew herself more and more to things below and beyond and in the final years of her life was in danger of losing her own self, together with the self known to those who loved her. Goethe's myth enacts the danger of such 'self'-destruction. The haunted female of Goethe's melodrama portrays a 'living soul' whose suffering is chthonic but strangely poetic. Her anxious quest is a way of sorrows, a *via dolorosa*, forcing her to live as never before – on the edge. One conclusion that can be drawn from this is that Cornelia's narcissistic behaviour may be understood as a psychological regression in the face of the harsh external world. Another reading masked in Goethe's adoption of a myth is the theme of painful human relations, whose pathos has demonstrably regained the initial tragic potential of the tale, where the conflict between a self-willed individual and social institutions, between passion and reason, is depicted as tragedy. Goethe's apprehension of the existential anguish portrayed in the Proserpina myth explores the hidden aspect of things, what exists 'beneath' – particularly the ruthless aspects of human need. As in *Werther*, Goethe's ability to produce emotions of the most agonizing kind is evident in his portrayal of *Proserpina*. The precarious condition in which women find themselves is here reinforced by Goethe in a personal light using a modern background to the tragic myth. The account, though confessional, should be taken in a broad ideological context as an account of a woman's condition echoing, in its own way, the general condition of women at that time.

Crossing the Threshold: From Mythology to Social Politics

Goethe's *Proserpina* dramatizes what Catherine Clement calls the 'undoing of women'.[48] The poet's preoccupation with what is, perhaps, 'the central mythic figure for women'[49] is part of Goethe's persistent concern with feminine identity. In *Proserpina* Goethe uses the past to demonstrate the historical reality of the present, especially related to cultural revisions desired by many women in the late eighteenth/early nineteenth century. His monodrama focuses on the resistance of Proserpina and is vitally concerned with the politics of power: how the marginalized gain a voice within a social system; how women achieve strong positive identities in a patriarchal culture. In his monodrama, Goethe deconstructs the traditional reading of the abduction of Proserpina, particularly the validation of social codes that permit and even sanction the destruction of women. Proserpina's lines bring to life the curtailment of women's control over their own destinies because of their vulnerability to physical and sexual abuse. His drama is a mythic exploration of the disenchantment that many women experience in patriarchal cultures, and exposes the damage caused to those who are forced to live by such reductive codes. Although at first reading Proserpina's story could be interpreted as an encoding of patriarchal violence – the story of Proserpina's rape is a chronicle of brute force legalized by the king of the universe in spite of a mother's opposition – behind this portrayal lies Goethe's acknowledgement of the wisdom of women: nothing is as important to Proserpina as reuniting with her mother, just as nothing is as important to Ceres as re-establishing her relationship with her daughter. Through the introduction of Ceres' and the nymphs' silence, Goethe reinforces the importance of such relationships. Goethe's heroine learns painfully that narcissism, as signified by her going off alone to pick the narcissus, leads to isolation from women and that only her bond with someone who values connectedness can save her from permanent death. Goethe's version of the myth, thereby, validates female standards of moral and social conduct, even implying the superiority of a relationship-based reality over rule-based reality.

The world represented in Goethe's *Proserpina* thus provides a fascinating mirror-image of nineteenth-century cultural history. Written in a period that marked the beginning of the bourgeoisie's consciousness of individual self-worth, Goethe's audience undoubtedly found much to appreciate in Proserpina's plight. Although Goethe uses an ancient myth he does not alienate his audience from reality because Proserpina voices contemporary issues and concrete social tensions. According to Diderot, a tableau ought to organize a picture depicting an authentic moment of nature, of truth.[50] Goethe's monodrama raises questions of identity and explores its breakdown in women, thus pointing the way towards modernism. In *Proserpina*, Goethe explores the effects of oppression and the toll it takes on a woman who seeks to redefine herself and her world. Like Gretchen, Goethe's heroine experiences a journey to an underworld that entails profound and traumatic change. The *doppelgänger* motif in Proserpina's dream (ll.14-28) presents an ideal image of herself. The beautiful maiden who appears in the dream presents a picture of normality and attractiveness. Part of the narrative effect hinges upon this dream sequence, when events happen out of sequence and images are fused in a way that seems logical yet cannot withstand conscious scrutiny. Proserpina's dream encompasses the conflict of her thoughts, as she struggles with the vision of self as Other and rebels against what is defined by the larger world as reason itself. Each melodramatic recitation, each metaphor explores these irreconcilables, as she rages against the values and expectations of a social order that has attempted to define her. Unlike the Greek and Roman representations, Goethe's Proserpina has no one who will negotiate a compromise for her, no one who will call her back from her inward journey. There is no revitalization at the end, no strong mother who will rescue this Proserpina figure from her entrapment. The complementary deities of

Ovid's tale are reduced, thereby increasing her isolation, and the destruction of her bower of bliss is permanent. By the end of the monodrama, she is a lost Proserpina, unreclaimed from hell. Like the wanderer in Schubert's *Winterreise*, she is left to cope with her 'madness' in isolation. That Proserpina rails against this fate in the final scenes of the melodrama maintains the dramatic tension to the end. In the final stanzas the listener is confronted by the shocking end of her mental and emotional journey –a dénouement that is neither psychologically nor socially acceptable.[51] Like many dramatizations before the 1830s, Goethe's melodrama charts these changes in socio-psychological terms, but fails to provide effective answers, true enlightenment, or permanent resolution – experience and reflection tell us that here we have been bequeathed a codified truth in art. Nonetheless Goethe's drama is persuasive and artistically satisfying. The questions are raised in performance, just as the human issues, like the myth, are repeated *ad infinitum*.

Goethe and the Art of German Melodrama

The invention of melodrama has been generally attributed to Jean Jacques Rousseau, who used the term 'mélodrame' as a synonym for opera, like the Italian *melodrama*. Rousseau's *Pygmalion* (1770), generally acknowledged as the first melodrama, was inspired by Rousseau's thesis that the French language did not lend itself to music theatre.[52] Ironically Rousseau had no intention of developing a new genre; as with *Devin du Village*, he saw *Pygmalion* as an example to illustrate his theoretical ideas and as a means of bringing a better degree of realism to music. The music for *Pygmalion*, partly composed by Rousseau and partly composed by the musical amateur, Horace Coignet, was first performed in Lyon in 1770. In this setting music played a subsidiary role: it remained confined by the imitation principle and followed the poetic declamation exactly. Two years later, two more successful renditions were composed by the Viennese composer, Franz Aspelmeyer and Anton Schweitzer, musical director of the Seyler theatrical company. The role of music was augmented in Schweitzer's setting, which was first performed in Weimar in May 1772. At Weimar, where the Seyler company were then playing, the actor in the title role, Johann Böck, won such acclaim for his performance that another member of the company, Johann Christian Brandes, decided to write a similar piece for his wife. His *Alceste* was premiered at Weimar on 28 May 1773 and followed by seven or eight performances of *Pygmalion* up to 3 August 1773. Goethe's reading of Rousseau's *Pygmalion* can be dated as early as 1773 because he refers to it as an 'excellent work' in a letter to Sophie von La Roche on 19 January 1773,[53] and in later years he wrote admiringly of it in *Dichtung und Wahrheit* (iii, 2).

The most prolific and successful of the many melodramatic composers was Georg (Jiri) Anton Benda (1722-1795), *Kapellmeister* of the Duke of Gotha. Benda is frequently recognized as the first composer to develop Rousseau's concept into highly artistic compositions that influenced his contemporaries. Benda insisted, however, that he composed his two most famous melodramas, *Ariadne in Naxos* (1775) and *Medea* (1775) – the latter arousing Mozart's interest – without any knowledge of Rousseu's *Pygmalion*. Musically Rousseau's work hardly played a role in shaping Benda's manner of composition. The original source of Benda's melodramas lies much more in the example of the Jesuit school in Jicin, whose syllabus contained classical rhetoric and music, and whose dramatic performances were of a melodramatic nature. It was Benda who wrote the most famous setting of *Pygmalion*,[54] which Goethe referred to as a 'small but peculiarly ground-breaking work'[55] and which Goethe still defended in his correspondence with Schiller in 1797. For Goethe, Benda's melodramas served as excellent examples of the old type, where the music and text usually alternate, and the comments of his librettist, Johannes Christian Brandes, are insightful:

> The composer has complete freedom in the overture...but, as soon as the play begins, the music must be subordinate to [the text] and may not interrupt it until the action requires a pause or until the actor is lost in contemplation or reflection. At this point the composer may allow his inspiration free reign...but he must never interrupt any word, any picture, or any striking occurrence with a bar of music...[Otherwise] the text will partially destroy the music and the music [will destroy] the text.[56]

The central idea of German melodrama is, therefore, to allow music an autonomous non-verbal presence that sometimes supports and sometimes competes with the words it accompanies, but always maintains a continuous musical presence.[57]

The experimental genre of melodrama generated its fair share of controversy in nineteenth-century Germany, primarily because this relation between music and declamation was indeterminate. With the connection of declamation and instrumental music, melodrama consummated the demands of the emotionalization of poetry through the music by combining the baroque rhetoric of *Affektdarstellung* (portrayal of emotions) with the individual-psychological language of the *Empfindsamkeit*. It also fulfilled the needs of the public for a serious *tragedia per musica*; by avoiding the forms of Italian opera, it also steered clear of the central problems of serious opera on the German stage. The omnipresent point of criticism of incomprehensible texts (because Italian and/or sung) and nonsensical texts was forgotten. Just as the central problem of the German travelling companies was the lack of capable singers, so melodramas were mainly written for the first tragic actress of an ensemble, who was, characteristically, an exceptional master of her subject. The reproach of 'unnatural' was, therefore, hardly levelled at the melodrama. Despite such achievements, contemporaries continued to attack melodrama as a monstrous aesthetic configuration, with Coleridge more interestingly recognizing it as a modern 'Jacobean drama'. Even Herder, who in the heyday of the melodrama had seen it as an ideal form and had written his *Brutus* for melodramatic setting in 1772, considered melodrama as 'a hybrid form, which does not blend; a dance, where the music lags behind; a speech with the music dwelling hard on its heels'.[58] After 1800, melodrama disappeared astonishingly quickly from the German stage. Its swift decline was connected with the improved education of German singers since the end of the 1780s; the reintegration of serious elements into opera; as well as the general strengthening of German opera and the decline of tragedy. Melodrama had profited, however, from a music-dramatic niche and from the aesthetic consideration of how strongly music can influence the semantics of speech.

Musical Mimesis and the Representation of Reality

Around the time when Goethe wrote *Proserpina*, the aesthetic reflections on German poetry and music theatre sought an ideal way of combining music and language. In the second half of the eighteenth century the ideals of the rationally dominated *Aufklärung* and the emotional movements of *Sturm und Drang* and *Empfindsamkeit* had increasingly sought to bring poetry and music closer together. Sentimental literature had already witnessed the paradigmatic shift from expression dominated by rationality to a 'sentimental' language or 'language of the heart', especially realized in lyric poetry. Although the expressive language of the poets also proved to be rash, it showed the boundaries of such intentions. While the language of poetry must also be an *Ideensprache* and *Verstandessprache*, music was increasingly recognized as the language which could arouse emotions, feelings and suffering with real immediacy. Even Gottsched – whose rejection of opera on the basis of its lack of life-like characters is sufficiently well-known – admitted 'that words that are sung to a suitable melody have a much stronger emotional effect'[59] and he was not completely averse to an integration of music into drama:

> So it remains to be asked whether, instead of the old choral ode, it would be possible to have an aria as we write them, or a cantata sung by several singers, but one which completely matched the preceding event and as a result introduced moral reflections. I, for my part, would be very much in favour of it.[60]

Despite Gottsched's aversion to opera, he hoped for a procedure which 'through an equal union of music and poetry, the dignity of the latter should be preserved without curtailment'.[61] Like many writers around him[62] Goethe was engaged by this aesthetic debate. What impressed Goethe most was the absolute confidence in music evinced by the theoretician of music aesthetics, Johann Mattheson, whose theoretical writing on the baroque *Affektenlehre* (theory of emotions) the poet greatly respected. As early as 1739 Mattheson had claimed:

> The main characteristics [of a prologue and intermezzo] consist of this: in a short [musical] idea and prologue a brief portrayal is given of what should follow. And so one can easily conclude that the emotions expressed must coincide with the same passions as are presented in the work itself. [63]

Mattheson's principle of musical imitation was a central concern in Goethe's music aesthetics. Goethe had followed the development of this debate into contemporary composition where a series of word-painting procedures were set forward, whereby non-musical occurrences were presented by musical means. While the 'objective' or common 'lower' tone-painting sought to mirror the sound of external events by means of instrumental imitation (for example the sound of thunder), the 'higher' tone-painters sought to arouse an aesthetic of association in the listener – to imitate the impression of thunder. In the Goethe-Zelter letters the first form of imitation was increasingly the target of criticism.[64] Goethe addressed Adalbert Schöpke's question for the first time on 16 February 1818 as to what the musician could paint in music:

> With regard to the question [...] as to what a musician can paint, I dare to answer with a paradox: nothing and everything. Nothing! What he perceives through the outer senses he can imitate; but he may portray *everything* that he *feels* through the working of these outer senses. To imitate [the sound of] thunder in music is not art, but the musician who makes me feel as if I was hearing thunder is to be valued. To capture the inner [feeling] in music without needing the outer means is music's greatest and most noble privilege.[65]

Goethe's exploration of the immediacy of the language of music was influenced by the general idea – rather than a strict application – of *Affektenlehre* in opera seria and the classical *Ethoslehre* (ethics) which touches on the idea that human emotions can be reproduced in musical form.[66] Goethe trusted the clarity of the psychological effect of music, which leads to a universal music language. Above all the poet recognized the emotional depth that music could add to speech, and the aesthetic aim of *Proserpina* was to emphasize what the words express, and to supply what they only imply or hint at: music being superior to speech in emotional expression.

Although the exploration of music and poetry in early melodrama was recognized as 'the most modern of all that is modern'[67] the early nineteenth-century composers of this form were, nevertheless, strongly influenced by the eighteenth-century classicist principle according to which each art must remain autonomous. Echoing this principle, Goethe warned, concerning his *Proserpina*, that confusion would result if the two arts of the melodrama were to be mingled: the music, he stressed, should be confined only to the function of cementing blocks of dialogue. Thinking similarly, most composers of melodrama – Rousseau, Benda, Mozart, Beethoven, and Mendelssohn – cultivated melodramas mainly of the old type. Like the later composers of melodrama, Goethe sought to mingle music and speech in his melodrama though only in restricted passages – unlike the extensive simultaneous usage of music and speech in later melodrama. With Eberwein, Goethe strove to create a 'Gefühlskunst', which would portray the elemental emotions through rhapsodic diction, an exploration of tone colours, and would mirror swift changes of emotion in an alternation of music and speech.[68] Goethe recognized Eberwein's music as essential to establishing and maintaining the emotional tone and overall tempo of the melodramatic action. In *Proserpina* the music accompanies incantations, transformations, and spectral apparitions; melodramatic music bridges the gaps between the invisible and the visible, the silent and the spoken, and the living and the dead. Goethe took full advantage of the enforced division between speech and music in contemporary melodrama to depict Proserpina's interaction with the spirit realm (for example, bars 319-32; 350-58). Eberwein's music underscores the furiously hypertense emotionality of the scene as Proserpina is torn between the horror of the present and memories of the past, between outbursts of despairing hatred and an almost sisterly turning towards the darkest mythological figures to be featured on the classical Weimar stage. Proserpina's melodramatic passages are at their most fantastic from bars 487ff., when the unsettling silence of Ceres and Jupiter initiates a sequence of melodramatic events that brings the work to its climax.

Intermezzo: Carl Eberwein's collaboration with Goethe

Carl Eberwein (1786-1868) commenced his musical studies under his father's direction, before joining the court orchestra first as flautist and later as first violinist (1803). Through this position Eberwein became acquainted with Goethe, who recognized potential in the young musician's talent. In 1807 the poet appointed him musical director for performances in his home and the following year he sent him for a two-year period of study with Carl Friedrich Zelter, from whom he would gain a solid foundation in compositional techniques.[69] On his return from Berlin, Eberwein was appointed chamber musician in the Ducal orchestra (1810) and in the Herderkirche (1810). Although he failed to secure the position of court *Kapellmeister* in 1817, he was appointed Director of Music and Opera at the court in 1826, a position he held until his retirement in 1849.

Eberwein is an important composer among Weimar's most eminent musicians, not only for his collaboration with Goethe but also for the role he played in the musical life at Weimar –a topic which recurs in his literary writing.[70] Apart from his close collaboration with Goethe on *Proserpina*, he composed numerous settings of the poet's texts, from settings of poems from Goethe's *West-östlicher Divan* to music for Goethe's *Faust* and some Singspiele to texts by the poet.

When Goethe returned to *Proserpina* in 1815, he did not go back to the music prepared by Seckendorff, he wanted a more modern score. Eberwein's setting leaves us in no doubt about that; it is as a contemporary of Spohr and Weber that he composes *Proserpina*. In the intensive collaboration which took place while the production was being prepared in January 1815, Goethe was also anticipating the idea of a *Gesamtkunstwerk*. He paid close attention to every aspect of the production, especially to its music, its costumes, gestures, and staging. When discussing contemporary settings of the poet's works, scholars often lapse into regret that Goethe did not have someone of his rank at his side for musical collaborations. Yet Eberwein's willingness to go along with Goethe's wishes was an advantage here: the selfless striving of the young composer to satisfy the poet's intentions and concrete instructions is everywhere apparent; it is the nearest thing we have to a composition by Goethe. In a letter to Zelter on 23 January 1815, Goethe wrote with enthusiasm, 'We've put some real heat into this little work, so that it can rise up like a balloon and can still explode like a firework',[71] and Eberwein never composed as interestingly as he did here.

Modes of Musical Discourse in Eberwein's and Goethe's *Proserpina*

Goethe's *Proserpina* has all the prerequisites of a good melodramatic text. It is written in verse rather than prose, which is more difficult to set melodramatically, using the nineteenth-century musical resource. Verse, on the other hand, with its regular metric patterns, was easier to synchronize with music than prose with its irregular rhythms. Goethe's text also abounds in mood and imagery which lends itself well to musical description. Goethe provides the work with a broad sectional frame: a free sonata form with four major sections – an exposition (ll.1-44, where Proserpina bemoans her fate), its modified restatement (ll.45-100), a development section (ll.101-197, where she calls to Ceres and Jupiter in hope), and a recapitulation with further motivic development where her fate is sealed (ll.198-216) – and an extensive coda (ll.217-72). However, the gradual mounting of the story and the music towards one central climax, along with the skilful metamorphosis of the motives, imbues the structure of this melodrama with a sense of dramatic continuity rather than that of a sectional form.

Goethe resolves the tension of music versus drama in a manner akin to that of traditional Italian opera by allowing the music and the text each in turn to dominate. Accordingly, Eberwein's music commands in the extensive passages where it serves to create mood. These consist of Eberwein's allegorical prologue (bars 1-259) and following Proserpina's chant of oppression where her fate is introduced – the work's *Grundgedanke* (fundamental idea) – Eberwein creates an Arcadian setting (bars 272-289) and three other shorter, intensely atmospheric instrumental passages (bars 319-324 and 326-332; bars 382-386 and bars 469-486). These three atmospheric passages are inserted at psychologically crucial moments of the story: the first, Proserpina's song of lamentation; the second when she calls on her mother and the portrayal of maternal and filial love is orchestrated at all levels (lyrical, musical, and visual) to move the audience to sympathy before the third, where her fate is sealed. The 'drama' on the other hand, dominates in five extensive passages of recitation answered by music: Proserpina's abduction (bars 260-71 and 298-318); Ceres' search for her daughter (bars 398-432); the renewal of hope (bars 455-468); tasting the forbidden fruit (bars 487-507), followed by Proserpina's renewed invocation, where the heroine's wrath finds its musical outlet in Eberwein's score (bars 520-27; 533-547 and 559-92). In all of these passages, scenes are set and narratives unfold. These purely verbal passages, which are inserted into the music, do not injure its structure, for Goethe places them in the four major structural sections of music. A good example of this is found in Eberwein's score for the finale where the dynamic principle of Goethe's text is given in an absence/presence dichotomy and Proserpina's presence is felt in her absence as the music keeps accusing her oppressor. The alternation of voice and orchestra initiates poignant cycles of tension that propel the music forward. As Proserpina redoubles her efforts, the music imitates her by redoubling its pace as the rhythms become increasingly rapid.

At the same time Goethe and Eberwein are able to introduce many short verbal interjections into the music again without destroying its flow. They accomplish this in two ways: either by placing the words directly after unresolved chords that are strong enough to require resolution even after the interruption (bars 369-81) or by shaping them in the manner of a narrative, with the familiar stereotyped chordal outbursts (bars 398-442). Similarly, the effective insertion of intense passages such as the procession of lost souls in hell (bars 333-49; 358-68) shows that the composer does not necessarily destroy the dramatic effect of a text, as many early composers of melodrama believed. Introduced at those psychologically crucial moments, such passages heighten rather than weaken the drama, while aiding the integration of music and text. Goethe and Eberwein construct those passages in which the words and the music are heard simultaneously also in two general ways: by allowing the music to prevail (bars 319-324; 382-86 and 469-86) or to be of equal importance to the text (bars 333-49). The first way produces a result for Goethe that is reminiscent of an aria, for the music is moulded into long attractive lyrical lines, where the individual words are less important than their general verbal context.

The Spirit of Goethe's Melodrama

Goethe's *Proserpina* bears testimony to the poet's intimate knowledge of German music theatre. Goethe's plot closely mirrors contemporary melodramatic forms, which stemmed mainly from Greek mythology or from the Roman circle of legends. Proserpina is the perfect protagonist of nineteenth-century melodrama, whose heroines traditionally resemble the static figures of baroque opera. In a hopeless situation they declaim their sorrow without hope of bettering their situation, without the possibility of independent action. Through a retrospective view into happier times, often childhood, and the call for help to parents, the text of a melodrama is generated that does without action and must manage without dialogue. Instead of the dramatic tension of dialogue and action, contrast is created within the structure of the protagonist's monologue, which generates the material for musical expression. Goethe's adaptation of the antique myth shares the tragic ending of the melodrama, which avoids the *lieto fine*[72] of opera serie and instead corresponds to a short tragedy, where the moment of *catharsis* fails in favour of excitement of emotions.

Part of the historical significance of Goethe's collaboration with Eberwein is the poet's recognition of the important role melodrama played in the cultural dynamics of the nineteenth century, a role that was downplayed or denied outright by most earlier critics. A reading of *Proserpina* that allows for a more complex interpretation of the performance and reception of the genre and for multiple and shifting perspectives in audience response, enables us to situate the melodrama as a crucial rather than a peripheral phenomenon of German cultural history.[73] Nineteenth-century melodrama served as a crucial space in which the cultural, political, and economic exigencies of the century were played out and transformed into public discourses about issues ranging from gender-specific dimensions of individual station and behaviour to the role and status of the 'nation' in local as well as imperial politics.[74] Goethe's use of the *Proserpina* myth to unmask these cultural dynamics points not only to the myth's structural malleability in voicing contemporary cultural issues, but also to the role it played in 'resolving' such hegemonic discourses. During the nineteenth century, 'woman' was central to the preoccupations of artists, despite her unassuming role in the social hierarchy. At the start of the Romantic movement the purveyors of '*la littérature de prostitution*' had attacked the principles that sustained existing family structures. They criticized the laws that made a woman a minor for life, subject first to the authority of her father and then her husband, without rights or property for herself. They demanded the re-establishment of divorce and supported a woman's rights to keep her children if she left her husband. In response the bourgeoisie lent its support to those authors who offered ideal images of woman. Despite her diminished status, many melodramas revolve around a woman: a man desires her; a man has abducted her; someone has taken a mother's child; she is expected to marry against her wishes – it is her emotions which give meaning to these episodes. So, too, violence is everywhere in the genre of melodrama: the heroine in disarray, terrorized by the gesture of a man who has abducted her, is a common figure. Goethe's *Proserpina*, therefore, mirrors the reactionary ideology of contemporary melodrama and is a fascinating interplay of intersecting cultural and ideological horizons. By enacting the complexities of women's roles in society Goethe enabled the audience to identify with the suffering of the heroine and to perceive such cultural tensions even though it may not have been able to translate them into active alternatives. In this light, the most significant element of Goethe's interpretation of the Proserpina story is the historical reconfiguration of Proserpina's fate, for the moral construct framed by this melodrama is society's responsibility to women. [75]

---

[1] The Greek version of the name is 'Persephone'; as Goethe has used Roman sources and Roman names, I use the Roman name, 'Proserpina', consistently through this article.

[2] Elizabeth T. Hayes, *Images of Persephone: Feminist Readings in Western Literature* (Florida: University Press of Florida 1994), ix.
[3] Barbara Walker has documented this in *The Women's Encyclopedia of Myths and Secrets* (San Francisco: Harper and Row, 1983), 786-87.
[4] Gian Lorenzo Bernini, *The Rape of Proserpina* (1621-1622), marble group (height 295cm), Galleria Borghese, Rome.
[5] Rembrandt's *The Abduction of Proserpina* (1630), Oil on Wood (83 x 78cm), Staatliche Museen Preussischer Kulturbesitz, Gemäldegalerie, Berlin.
[6] Claudio Giovanni Antonio Monteverdi, *Proserpina rapita* (1630), libretto by Giulio Strozzi. Another musical representation from this time is Pompeo Colonna's setting of Casteli's text in 1645.
[7] Jean Baptiste Lully, *Proserpine* (1680 & 1707), libretto by Phillipe Quinault, after Ovid. In 1803 Nicolas-François created a three-act version of Quinault's libretto for music by Paisello; it is unlikely that Goethe knew this work as it had only thirteen performances and an Italian adaptation made in 1806-08 was never performed. Nor are Lully's or Pompeo Colona's Proserpina (1645) among Goethe's collection of libretti.
[8] Serge Pitou, *The Paris Opera: An Encyclopedia of Operas, Ballets, Composers and Performers. Rococo and Romantic, 1715-1815* (Westport, Conn.: Greenwood Press, 1983), 450-51. Alfred Lowenberg, *Annals of Opera* 3rd edn (Geneva: Societas Bibliographia, 1978).
[9] Stravinsky's *Persephone* (1933): 'The Abduction of Persephone', 'Persephone in the Underworld', and 'Persephone Reborn'.
[10] *Hymn to Demeter*, English translation by Andrew Lang, *The Homeric Hymns* (London: George Allen, 1899), 184. The term Homeric does not necessarily ascribe authorship to the poet Homer, but rather indicates that the poem is in Homeric style.
[11] Another early recorded version of the tale, also from the classical period, is found in Hesiod's *Theogony*.
[12] Stephen Hinds, *The Metamorphosis of Persephone: Ovid and the Self-conscious Muse* (Cambridge: Cambridge University Press, 1987), 56.
[13] See, for example. John Milton, *Paradise Lost* (London: Macmillan and Co., 1962), Book IV, v.267-272, 10.
[14] Percy Bysshe Shelley (*Song of Proserpine,* 1839); Algernon Charles Swinburne (*Hymn to Proserpine*, 1866 and *The Garden of Proserpine*, 1866); Dante Gabriel Rossetti (*Proserpina*, 1880); George Meredith (*The Day of the in Hades*, 1883 and *The Appeasement of Demeter*, 1887); Alfred Lord Tennyson (*Demeter and Persephone in Enna*, 1887); Heinrich Heine (*Unterwelt*, 1844); Oscar Wilde (*Ravenna, Charmide, The Burden of Itys, The Garden of Eros*, and *Theocritus: A Villanelle*, collected in *Poems*, 1881); D.H. Lawrence (*Bavarian Gentians*, 1932 and *Purple Anemones*, 1931); Robert Bridges (*Demeter, A Masque*, 1904); Eavan Boland (*The Pomegranate*, 1994). For a full survey of the literary tradition of the myth, see N.J. Richardson, ed., *The Homeric Hymn to Demeter* (Oxford, 1974), 68-86.
[15] Jean Pierre Vernant, *Myth and Society in Ancient Greece* trans. Janet Lloyd (London: Methuen & Co., 1982), 219.
[16] Walter Pater, *Greek Studies* (London: Macmillan and Co., 1910), 91.

[17] The location of the Greek myth is Mount Nysa. In Goethe's *Proserpina* there is no direct reference to the Sicilian landscape, but the poet's knowledge of Ovid's *Metamorphoses* and his recognition of Sicily as the ideal landscape of Poussin's paintings suggests the Sicilian Lakes of Pergus as Goethe's setting.

[18] In Ovid, Cyane and Arethusa, Naiads to the River God, Alpheus, are the two nymphs attending on Proserpine. In Greek mythology Artemis (Diane, the Moon Goddess) and Athena (Minerva, the Goddess of Wisdom) are Proserpina's most conspicuous companions on the Nysian Plain. In other versions, Ino and Iris appear.

[19] Alpheus is the River God, whose river disappears underground. Samuel Taylor Coleridge's famous depiction of the river in the opening lines of poem, 'Kubla Khan', comes to mind: 'In Xanadu did Khubla Khan/ A stately pleasure-dome decree, /Where Alph, the sacred river, ran /Through caverns measureless to man, /Down to a sunless sea' (ll.1-5).

[20] As Jupiter's and Ceres's brother, Pluto was also Proserpina's uncle. Proserpina, therefore, became Queen of the Underworld and, by Pluto, mother of the Furies.

[21] The flowers vary according to the version: in the 'Homeric Hymn to Demeter', for example, Proserpina is gathering irises, hyacinths, and narcissi, flowers of spring; in Milton they are violets and lilies.

[22] In some versions of the tale, Proserpina plucks the fruit herself and it is Ascalaphus who tells Pluto that Proserpina has partaken of a pomegranate when Pluto had given her permission to return. In revenge Proserpina turned him into an owl by sprinkling him with the water of Phlegethon.

[23] Nicholas Boyle, *Goethe: The Poet and the* Age: *The Poetry of Desire, 1749-90*, vol. 1 (Oxford: Oxford University Press, 1992),.314. For further readings of this interpretation, see *FA* I, vol. 6, 949.

[24] *HA*, vol. 4, 665.

[25] Louise's birthday is 30 January; the celebratory performance took place the following day.

[26] *WA* VI, vol. 3. 174.

[27] Wilhelm Bode, *Die Tonkunst in Goethes Leben*, 2 vols (Berlin: Mittler, 1912), 80. 'ein Festspiel mit Gesängen und Tänzen'.

[28] *FA* I, vol. 6, 953. Because 'freventlich in den Triumph der Empfindsamkeit eingeschaltet [...] ihre Wirkung vernichtet [wurde]'.

[29] See, for example, Goethe to Zelter, 23 January 1815; Zelter to Goethe, 16 to 22 April 1815; Goethe to Zelter, 17 May 1815.

[30] Margherite Cottone, 'Kore', *Nuove Effemeridi, Goethe e I miti greci*, XIII, 52 (2000), IV, 23-29.

[31] Walter Pater, *Greek Studies*, p.109.

[32] Goethe's association of Proserpina with the moon is part of her literary heritage. In Chaucer's 'Knight's Tale', for example, he combines three aspects of the triple goddess Diana-Lucina-Proserpina: on earth she is Diana, the chaste goddess of the woodlands; above she is Lucina, the bright moon goddess protecting women from the pains of childbirth; and below, she is Proserpina, Queen of the Underworld. See Chaucer, *The House of Fame*, in *The Riverside Chaucer*, ed. Larry D. Benson, 3rd edn (Boston: Houghton Mifflin, 1987), 366, lines 1510-12.

[33] In Ovid's *Metamorphoses* Athena discovers and reports Proserpina's whereabouts to Ceres.

34 The phrase is Hugh Parry's in 'Ovid's *Metamorphoses*: Violence in a Pastoral Landscape', *TAPA* 95 (1964), 274.

35 Cornelia Goethe (1750-1777). For socio-historical interpretations of her life, examining the restrictive role of women in the eighteenth century, see Christoph Michel, 'Cornelia in *Dichtung und Wahrheit. Kritisches zu einem Spiegelbild*', *Jahrbuch des deutschen Hochstifts* (1979); Ernst Beutler, 'Die Schwester Cornelia', *Ergänzungsband der Goethe Gedenkausgabe* (Zurich, 1960), 187-245; and Hans Schoofs' *Cornelia Goethe. Briefe und Correspondance Secrète* 1767-1769 (Darmstadt: Kore, Verlag Truate Hensch, 1990). From a psychological point of view, her life has been analysed by Otto Rank in 'Goethes Schwesterliebe', *Geschlecht und Gesellschaft* 9 (1914) and Karl R. Eissler in his *Goethe. A Psychoanalytic Study*, 2 vols (Detroit: Wayne University Press, 1963); Ulrike Prokop, 'Cornelia Goethe' in Luise F. Pusch and Judith Offenbach, *Schwestern berühmter Männer. Zwölf biographische Portraits* (Frankfurt: Insel Verlag, 1985); and Luise F. Pusch and André Banul, *Goethe an Cornelia: die 13 Briefe an seine Schwester* (Hamburg: Hoffmann and Campe, 1986). Sigrid Damm, *Cornelia Goethe* (Frankfurt: Insel Verlag, 1987) offers a general background on various aspects of Cornelia Goethe's life and letters and Ulrike Prokop's *Die Illusion vom Grossen Paar, Das Tagebuch der Cornelia Goethe*, vol. 2 (Frankfurt am Main: Fischer Taschenbuch Verlag, 1991) interprets her life against a background of gender studies.

36 Johann Wolfgang von Goethe, *Dichtung und Wahrheit, Goethes Werke. Hamburger Ausgabe*, ed. Erich Trunz, 14 vols (Munich: C.H. Beck Verlag, 1994), IX, 337.

37 Cornelia Goethe, Letter to Caroline Herder, 13 December 1773, in Witkowski, *Cornelia. Die Schwester Goethes* (Frankfurt/M.Literarische Anstalt Rütten u. Loening, 1903), 234. 'alle meine Hoffnungen, alle meine Wünsche sind nicht nur erfüllt –sondern weit – weit übertroffen. – Wen Gott lieb hat dem geb er so einen Mann'.

38 Johann Georg Schlosser, Letter to Lavater, 6 November 1773. Ibid, 83. 'Meine Geliebte ist nun meine Frau! Die schönste Weiber-Seele, die ich mir wünschen konnte: edel, zärtlich, gerade! Eine Frau, wie ich sie haben musste, um glücklich zu seyn.'

39 Johann Peter Eckermann, *Gespräche mit Goethe* (Stuttgart, Reclam, 1994), 28 March 1831, 508. ' [...] sie stand sittlich sehr hoch und hatte nicht die Spur von etwas Sinnlichem. Der Gedanke, sich einem Mann hinzugeben, war ihr widerwärtig, und man mag denken, dass aus dieser Eigenheit in der Ehe manche unangenehme Stunde hervorging.'

40 'ihr ekelt vor meiner Liebe'. See also Johann Georg Schlosser, *Eine Ehestandsscene* in Witkowski, *Cornelia. Die Schwester Goethes*, 104.

41 Cornelia Goethe, Letter to Auguste Gräfin Stolberg, 10 December 1776, in Witkowski, *Cornelia, Die Schwester Goethes*, 243. 'Ihre häusliche Glückseeligkeit ahnde ich und wünschte als Schwester unter Ihnen aufgenommen zu seyn, das ist der eine von den Wünschen, der nie erfüllt werden wird, denn unsere gegenseitige Entfernung ist so gross, dass ich nicht einmal hoffen darf, Sie jemals in diesem Leben zu sehen. Wir sind hier ganz allein, auf 30-40 Meilen weit ist kein Mensch zu finden; – meines Manns Geschäffte erlauben ihm nur sehr wenige Zeit bey mir zuzubringen, und da schleiche ich denn ziemlich langsam durch die Welt, mit einem Körper der nirgend hin als das Grab taugt. Der Winter ist mir immer unangenehm und beschwerlich, hier macht die schöne Natur unsre einzige Freude aus, und wenn die schläft schläft alles'.

42 Goethe, *Tagebuch*, 16 June 1777. 'Dunckler zerrissner Tag.'

43 Goethe, To his mother, Katherina Elizabeth Goethe, 16 November 1777, *WA*, IV, 3, 186. 'Mit meiner Schwester ist mir so eine starcke Wurzel die mich an der Erde hielt abgehauen worden, dass die Äste, von oben, die davon Nahrung hatten auch absterben müssen.'

44 Goethe, To Augusta Stolberg, 17 July 1777, *WA*, IV, 3, 165. 'Alles geben Götter die unendlichen/ Ihren Lieblingen ganz/ Alle Freuden die unendlichen/ Alle Schmerzen die unendlichen ganz.'

45 Jakob Michael Reinhold Lenz, *Die Moralische Bekehrung eines Poeten, von ihm selbst aufgeschrieben*, in *Goethe-Jahrbuch* 10 (Weimar: Böhlau, 1889), 46ff. 'Engel des Himmels', 'Abgott meiner Vernunft und meines Herzens zusammen', 'Beruhigung und Ziel aller meiner Wünsche'.

46 *Dichtung und Wahrheit, Goethes Werke, HA*, 10, 132. 'Sie besaß alles, was ein solcher höherer Zustand verlangt; ihr fehlt, was die Welt unerläßlich forderte.'

47 *Dichtung und Wahrheit, Goethe Werke, HA*, 9, 228-29. Ungern spreche ich dies im allgemeinen aus, was ich vor Jahren darzustellen unternahm, ohne daß ich es hätte ausführen können. Da ich dieses geliebte unbegreifliche Wesen nur zu bald verlor, fühlte ich genugsamen Anlaß, mir ihren Wert zu vergegenwärtigen, und so entstand bei mir der Begriff eines dichterischen Ganzen, in welchem es möglich gewesen wäre, ihre Individualität darzustellen: allein es ließ sich dazu keine andere Form denken als die der Richardsonschen Romane. Nur durch das genauste Detail, durch unendliche Einzelnheiten, die lebendig alle den Charakter des Ganzen tragen und, indem sie aus einer wundersamen Tiefe hervorspringen, eine Ahndung von dieser Tiefe geben; nur auf solche Weise hätte es einigermaßen gelingen können, eine Vorstellung dieser merkwürdigen Persönlichkeit mitzuteilen: denn die Quelle kann nur gedacht werden, insofern sie fließt. Aber von diesem schönen und frommen Vorsatz zog mich, wie von so vielen anderen, der Tumult der Welt zurück, und nun bleibt mir nichts übrig, als den Schatten jenes seligen Geistes nur, wie durch Hülfe eines magischen Spiegels, auf einen Augenblick heranzurufen.'

48 Catherine Clement, *Opera, or the Undoing of Women*, trans. Betsy Wing (Minneapolis: University of Minnesota Press, 1988).

49 Susan Gubar, 'Mother, Maiden and the Marriage of Death: Women Writers and an Ancient Myth', *Women Studies* 6 (1979), 302.

50 Peter Szondi, 'Tableau and Coup de Théâtre: On the Social Psychology of Diderot's Bourgeois Tragedy', *On Textual Understanding and Other Essays*, trans. Harvey Mendelssohn, foreward Michael Hays (Minneapolis: University of Minnesota Press: 1986), 116.

51 Goethe's *Proserpina* is the opposite to Sandra M. Gilbert and Susan Gubar's category of the angel-woman who frequented many nineteenth-century literary works: a saintly angel, selfless and above all, revered for her silence. See Sandra M. Gilbert and Susan Gubar, *The Madwoman in the Attic: The Woman Writer and the Nineteenth-Century Literary Imagination* (New Haven and London: Yale University Press, 1984), 24-27.

52 Tina Hartmann, *Goethes Musiktheater. Singspiele, Opern, Festspiele, Faust* (Tübingen: Max Niemeyer Verlag, 2004).

53 *FA* II, vol. 1, 285. 'treffliche Arbeit'.

[54] Benda's *Pygmalion* was first performed in the Court Theatre at Gotha on 20 September 1779.

[55] *Dichtung und* Wahrheit, FA I, vol.14, 533. A 'kleinen aber merkwürdig Epoche machenden Werks'.

[56] The scholarly edition of Benda's *Ariadne auf Naxos* from which these comments are drawn was prepared by Alfred Einstein, 1920 (viii); see also Johann Christian Brandes, *Sämtliche dramatische Schriften*, vol. 1, xxvii ff.

[57] For further reading, see Peter Branscombe's article on 'Melodrama', *New Grove Dictionary of Music and Musicians, Grove Music Online* (Oxford: Oxford University Press, 2007).

[58] Herder, *Adrastea* (1803). *Viertes Stück Tanz und Melodrama, Werke* (1877-1913L §967/68), vol. 23, 329ff. 'Ein Mischspiel, das sich nicht mischt, ein Tanz, dem die Musik hintennach, eine Rede, der die Töne spähend auf die Fersen treten'.

[59] Johann Christoph Gottsched, *Versuch einer Critischen Dichtkunst.* (Leipzig, 1751; reprint Darmstadt: Wissenschaftliche Buchgesellschaft, 1962), 69. 'Daß Worte, die nach einer geschickten Melodey gesungen werden, noch viel kräftiger in die Gemüther wirkten.'

[60] Gottsched (1751, rpt. 1962), 624. 'So fraget sichs, ob es nicht möglich wäre, anstatt der alten Oden des Chores, eine nach unserer Art eingerichte Arie, oder Cantate, von etlichen Sängern, absingen zu lassen; aber eine solche, die sich allezeit zu der kurz zuvor gespielten Begebenheit schickte, und folglich moralische Betrachtungen darüber anstellte? Ich meinerseits wäre sehr dafür'.

[61] Cited in Ulrike Küster, *Das Melodrama. Zum ästhetikgeschichtlichen Zusammenhang von Dichtung und Wahrheit im 18. Jahrhundert* (Frankfurt am Main, Berlin, New York, Paris, Wien: Lang, 1994), 74. 'durch die einheitliche Verbindung von Musik und Poesie die Würde der letzten ungeschmälert bewahren [...] sollte'.

[62] See for example, Gotthold Ephraim Lessing, *Werke, Hamburgische Dramaturgie*, vol. 2 (Frankfurt am Main: Insel Verlag 1967), 228-29.

[63] Johann Mattheson, *Der vollkommene Capellmeister* (Hamburg: Christian Herold, 1739), 234. 'Ihre [die Vor- und Zwischenspiele] Haupt-Eigenschaft bestehet darin, daß sie in einem kurzen Begriff und Vorspiel eine kleine Abbildung desjenigen machen, so nachfolgen soll. Und da kann man leicht schliessen, daß die Ausdrückung der Affecten sich nach denjenigen Leidenschafften richten müsse, die im Wercke selbst hervorragen.'

[64] See Goethe to Zelter, 2 May 1820. A contemporary example of this debate is Reichardt's criticism of the 'Abknippen der Töne auf der Violine' to portray the nailing to the cross in favour of Hiller's *Sturmsymphonie* in *Die Jagd*, whose music did not imitate the sound of the wind, but evoked the sentiment of a storm in the listeners, Reichardt (1774: rpt. 1974), 115.

[65] *WA* IV, vol.29, 53-54. 'Auf die Frage [...] was der Musiker malen dürfe? wage ich mit einem Paradox zu antworten Nichts und Alles. Nichts! Wie er es durch die äußeren Sinne empfängt darf er nachahmen; aber Alles darf er darstellen was er bei diesen äußeren Sinneseinwirkungen empfindet. Den Donner in Musik nachzuahmen ist keine Kunst, aber der Musiker, der das Gefühl in mir erregt, als wenn ich donnern hörte würde sehr schätzbar sein [...] das Innere in Stimmung zu setzen, ohne die gemeinen äußern Mittel zu brauchen ist der Musik großes und edles Vorrecht.'

66 Descartes had already presented this idea in his text, 'Traité des passions de l'âme', in 1649.

67 Einstein's introduction to *Ariadne* 1920, viii.

68 Rudolph Gerber: 'Deutschland', *Die Musik in Geschichte und Gegenwart*, ed. Friedrich Blume, vol. 3 (Kassel and Basel: Bärenreiter Verlag, 1949-1986), 328.

69 Eberwein studied with Zelter for six weeks in 1808 (19 August to 30 September 1808) took eight months leave the following year (16 February 1809 to 23 October 1809). In between these two visits he regularly sent his compositions to Zelter, who monitored his progress. Eberwein's musical development is traced in the Goethe-Zelter correspondence. See GZ 6 April to 7 May 1808; GZ 22 June 1808; ZG 9-11 September 1808; GZ 19 September 1808; ZG 30 September to 15 October 1808; GZ 30 October 1808; GZ 7 November 1808; ZG 12 November 1808; GZ 16 February 1809; ZG 9 February 1809; GZ 1 June 1809; ZG 12 June to 14 July 1809; GZ 26 August 1809; GZ 16 September 1809; ZG 11-23 October; GZ 21 December 1809; ZG 30 December to 26 January 1810; GZ 18 March 1811. ZG 16-22 April 1815; GZ 17 May 1815; GZ 8 June 1816; ZG 16 June 1816; ZG: 26-27 July 1816; GZ 11 May 1820; ZG 21 May 1820; ZG 7 to 9 June 1820; ZG 8 to 13 August 1821; GZ 14 October 1821; GZ 8 March 1824; ZG 11-14 July; GZ 8 August 1826; ZG: 4 August 1828.

70 For further reading, see M. Zeigert, 'Goethe und der Musiker Karl Eberwein', *Berichte des freien deutschen Hochstiftes zu Frankfurt* (Frankfurt, 1836) and Wilhelm Bode, *Goethes Schauspieler und Musiker: Erinnerungen von Eberwein und Lobe* (Berlin: Mittler, 1912). Eberwein's collaboration with Goethe is also recorded in Wilhelm Bode, *Die Tonkunst in Goethes Leben* (Berlin: Mittler, 1912) and H.J. Moser, *Goethe und die Musik* (Leipzig: C.F. Peters, 1949).

71 Lorraine Byrne Bodley, *Goethe and Zelter: Musical Dialogues* (Aldershot: Ashgate, 2008), Letter no. 176; *MA* 20.1, 364.

72 The sudden turn of events, where everything is resolved at the last moment and a happy ending ensues.

73 Among the studies that have claimed to anchor melodrama to a specific historic context, Peter Brooks's *The Melodramatic Imagination: Balzac, Henry James, Melodrama, and the Mode of Excess* (New York: Columbia, rpt. 1995) can probably be singled out as the one that has had the most consequential impact. See also Elizabeth T. Hayes, ed., *Images of Persephone: Feminist Readings in Western Literature* (Florida: University Press of Florida, 1994).

74 Michael Hays and Anastasia Nikolopoulou, *Melodrama: The Cultural Emergence of a Genre* (New York: St Martin's Press, rpt. 1999), viii.

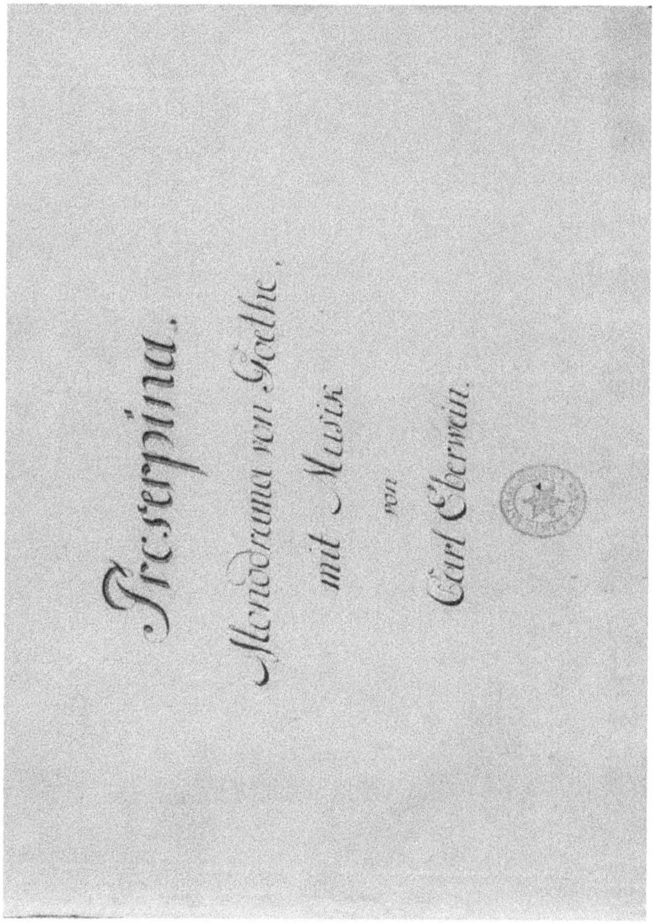

Figure 1: Title page of Eberwein's fair copy of Goethe's *Proserpina* (GSA 32/61)
Reproduced with permission of the Goethe- und Schiller-Archiv, Weimar.
(Photograph: ©Klassik Stiftung Weimar)

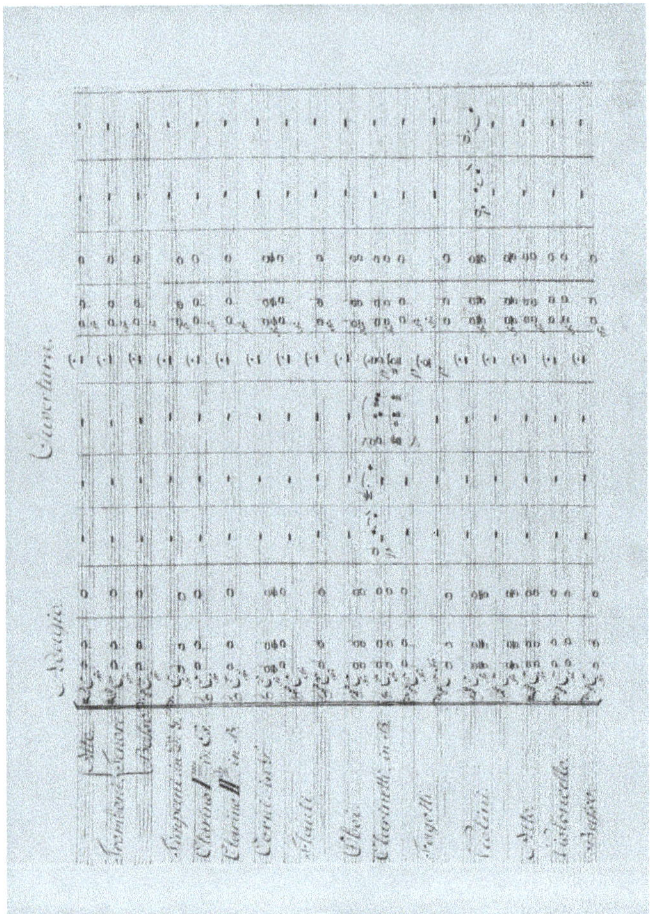

Figure 2: Eberwein's fair copy of Goethe's *Proserpina*, Overture, p.1 (GSA 32/61). Reproduced with permission of the Goethe- und Schiller-Archiv, Weimar. (Photograph: ©Klassik Stiftung Weimar)

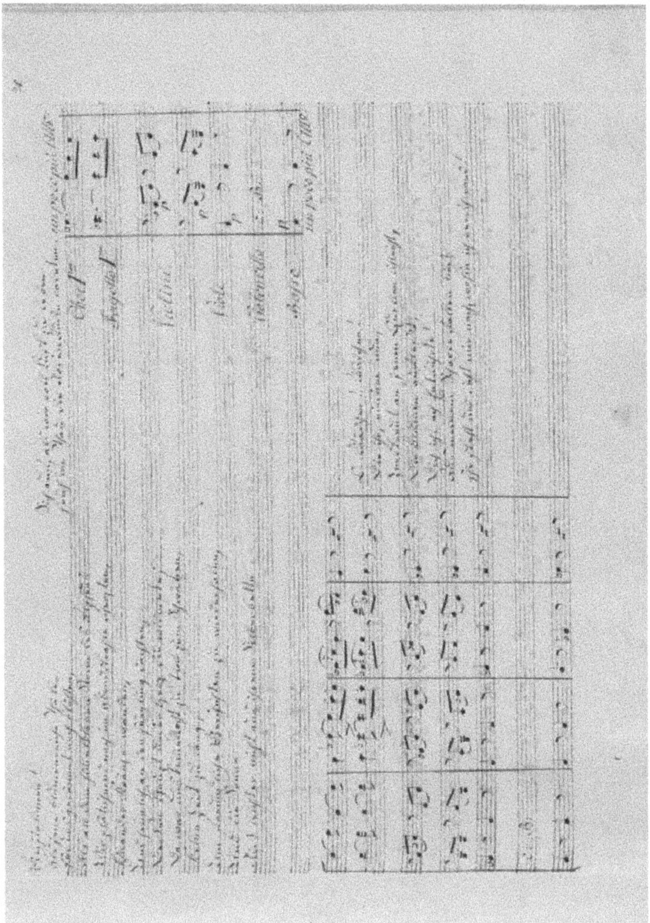

Figure 3: Eberwein's fair copy of Goethe's *Proserpina*, Melodrama, p.21 (GSA 32/61). Reproduced with permission of the Goethe- und Schiller-Archiv, Weimar. (Photograph: ©Klassik Stiftung Weimar)

Proserpina

Goethe's Melodrama
Music by Carl Eberwein

Orchestral Score & Translation

Instrumentation

2 flutes

2 oboes

2 Clarinets in B flat (doubling Clarinets in A)

2 Bassoons

2 French Horns in F

2 Trumpets in C

2 Tenor Trombones

1 Bass Trombone

Timpani

Strings

First Performance,

4 February 1815, Weimar.

Proserpina: Amalie Wolff.

First Performance of this score:

30 November 2007, National Concert Hall, Dublin

performed by the National Symphony Orchestra,

RTÉ Philharmonic Choir (director: Mark Duley),

Proserpina: Elfi Hoppe.

Conductor: Gerhard Markson.

Johann Wolfgang von Goethe
(1749 - 1832)

Proserpina

Carl Eberwein
(1786 - 1868)

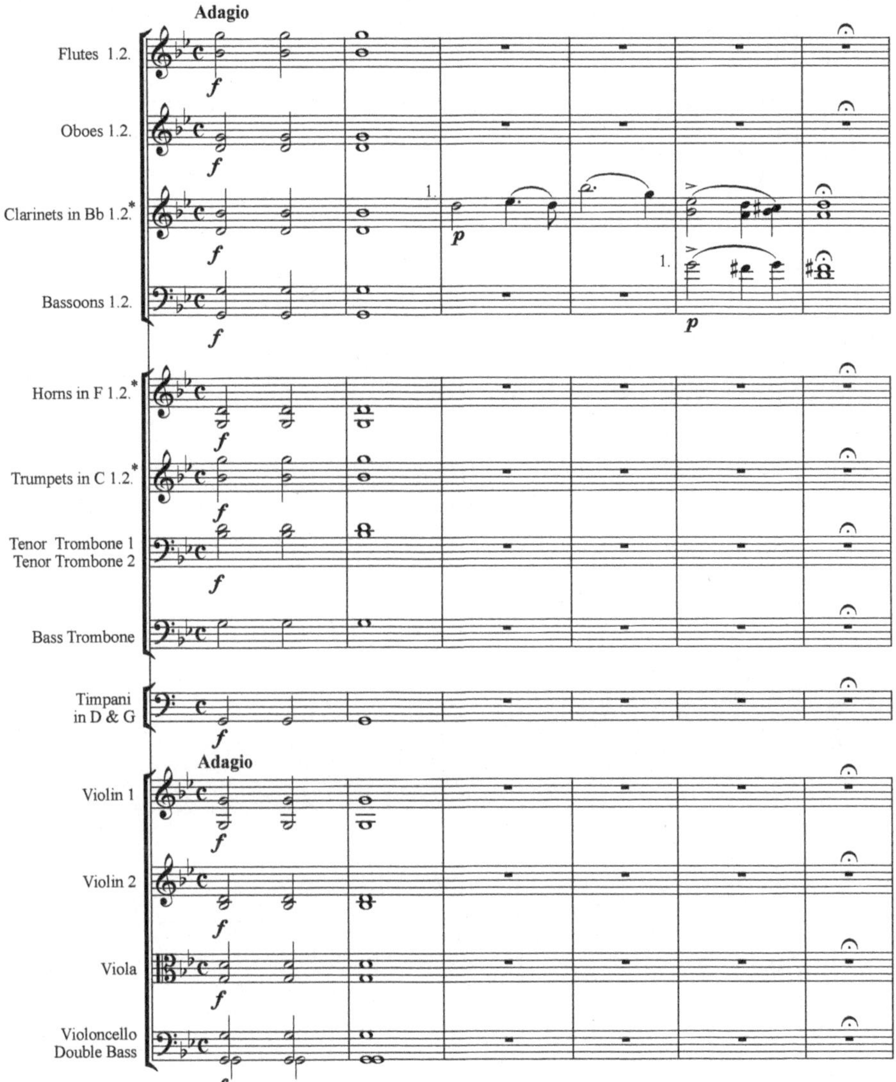

*suoni reali

7
Fl.
Ob.
Cl.
Bsn.
Hn.
Tpt.
Ten. Tbn. 1.
Ten. Tbn. 2.
Bass Tbn.
Timp.
Vln. I
Vln. II
Vla.
Vc.
Db.

13
Fl.
Ob.
Cl.
Bsn.
Hn.
Tpt.
Ten. Tbn. 1.
Ten. Tbn. 2.
Bass Tbn.
Timp.
Vln. I
Vln. II
Vla.
Vc.
Db.
p
p
1.
p
p

19
Fl.
Ob.
Cl.
Bsn.
a2
Hn.
a2
Tpt.
Ten. Tbn. 1.
Ten. Tbn. 2.
Bass Tbn.
Vln. I
Vln. II
Vla.
Vc.
Db.

22
Fl.
Ob.
Cl.
Bsn.
1.
Hn.
Tpt.
Ten. Tbn. 1.
Ten. Tbn. 2.
Bass Tbn.
Timp.
Vln. I
Vln. II
Vla.
Vc.
Db.

25
Fl.
Ob.
Cl.
Bsn.
Hn.
Tpt.
Ten. Tbn. 1.
Ten. Tbn. 2.
Bass Tbn.
Timp.
Vln. I
Vln. II
Vla.
Vc.
Db.
p
sfp
2.
tr

29
Fl.
Ob.
Cl.
Bsn.
Hn.
Tpt.
Ten. Tbn. 1.
Ten. Tbn. 2.
Bass Tbn.
Timp.
Vln. I
Vln. II
Vla.
Vc.
Db.
sfp
(tr)
pp

33
Allegro assai
Vln. I
Vln. II
Vc.
Db.
p
38
Vln. I
Vln. II
Vc.
Db.
42
Adagio
Vln. I
Vln. II
Vc.
Db.
p

Tempo I°
47
Fl.
Ob.
Cl.
Bsn.
a2
Hn.
Tpt.
Ten. Tbn. 1.
Ten. Tbn. 2.
Bass Tbn.
Timp.
Tempo I°
Vln. I
Vln. II
Vla.
Vc.
Db.

52
Fl.
Ob.
Cl.
Bsn.
a2
Hn.
Tpt.
Ten. Tbn. 1.
Ten. Tbn. 2.
Bass Tbn.
Vln. I
Vln. II
Vla.
Vc.
Db.

57
Fl.
Ob.
Cl.
Bsn.
Hn.
Tpt.
Ten. Tbn. 1.
Ten. Tbn. 2.
Bass Tbn.
Vln. I
Vln. II
Vla.
Vc.
Db.

62
Fl.
Ob.
Cl.
Bsn.
Hn.
Tpt.
Ten. Tbn. 1.
Ten. Tbn. 2.
Bass Tbn.
Vln. I
Vln. II
Vla.
Vc.
Db.

67
Fl.
Ob.
Cl.
Bsn.
Hn.
Tpt.
Ten. Tbn. 1.
Ten. Tbn. 2.
Bass Tbn.
Vln. I
Vln. II
Vla.
Vc.
Db.
sf

70
Fl.
Ob.
Cl.
Bsn.
a2
Hn.
Tpt.
Ten. Tbn. 1.
Ten. Tbn. 2.
Bass Tbn.
Vln. I
Vln. II
Vla.
Vc.
Db.
sf

74
Fl.
Ob.
Cl.
1. solo
Bsn.
Tpt.
Ten. Tbn. 1.
Ten. Tbn. 2.
Bass Tbn.
Vln. I
Vln. II
Vla.
Vc.
Db.

80
Cl.
Vln. I
Vln. II
Vla.
Vc.
Db.
86
Cl.
Vln. I
Vln. II
Vla.
Vc.
Db.

89
Cl.
Vln. I
Vln. II
Vla.
Vc.
Db.
93
Cl.
Tpt.
pp
Vln. I
Vln. II
Vla.
Vc.
Db.

99
1.
Fl.
f
1.
Ob.
f
Cl.
f
a2
Bsn.
f
Hn.
Tpt.
f
Ten. Tbn. 1.
Ten. Tbn. 2.
f
Bass Tbn.
f
Vln. I
f
Vln. II
f
Vla.
f
Vc.
Db.
f

104
1.
Fl.
Ob.
Cl.
Bsn.
Hn.
Tpt.
Ten. Tbn. 1.
Ten. Tbn. 2.
Bass Tbn.
Vln. I
Vln. II
Vla.
Vc.
Db.

109
Fl.
Ob.
Cl.
f
Bsn.
Hn.
Tpt.
Ten. Tbn. 1.
Ten. Tbn. 2.
Bass Tbn.
Timp.
Vln. I
Vln. II
Vla.
Vc.
Db.

112
Fl.
Ob.
Cl.
Bsn.
Hn.
Tpt.
Ten. Tbn. 1.
Ten. Tbn. 2.
Bass Tbn.
Timp.
Vln. I
Vln. II
Vla.
Vc.
Db.

114
Fl.
Ob.
Cl.
Bsn.
Hn.
f
Tpt.
Ten. Tbn. 1.
Ten. Tbn. 2.
Bass Tbn.
Timp.
f
Vln. I
Vln. II
Vla.
Vc.
Db.

119
Fl.
Ob.
Cl.
Bsn.
Hn.
Tpt.
Ten. Tbn. 1.
Ten. Tbn. 2.
Bass Tbn.
Timp.
Vln. I
Vln. II
Vla.
Vc.
Db.
a2
a 2
sf

124
Bsn.
Ten. Tbn. 1.
Ten. Tbn. 2.
Bass Tbn.
Vln. I
Vln. II
Vla.
Vc.
Db.
130
Vln. I
Vln. II
Vla.
Vc.
Db.

136
Vln. I
Vln. II
Vla.
Vc.
Db.
fp
fp
fp
fp

141
1. solo
Fl.
p
Vln. I
fp
Vln. II
fp
Vla.
fp
Vc.
Db.
f
p

145
Fl.
1.solo
Ob.
p
Cl.
1. solo
Bsn.
p
Hn.
Tpt.
Ten. Tbn. 1.
Ten. Tbn. 2.
Bass Tbn.
Timp.
Vln. I
fp
Vln. II
fp
Vla.
fp
Vc.
Db.
f
p

149
Fl.
Ob.
1. solo
Cl.
p
Bsn.
p
Hn.
Tpt.
p
Ten. Tbn. 1.
Ten. Tbn. 2.
Bass Tbn.
Timp.
Vln. I
Vln. II
Vla.
Vc.
Db.

154
Fl.
Ob.
(1.)
Cl.
1.
Bsn.
Hn.
2.
Tpt.
Ten. Tbn. 1.
Ten. Tbn. 2.
Bass Tbn.
Timp.
Vln. I
Vln. II
Vla.
Vc.
Db.

158
2.
Fl.
Ob.
Cl.
Bsn.
Hn.
Tpt.
Ten. Tbn. 1.
Ten. Tbn. 2.
Bass Tbn.
Timp.
Vln. I
Vln. II
Vla.
Vc.
Db.

(1.)
161
Fl.
(1.)
Ob.
Bsn.
164
Fl.
Ob.
1.
Bsn.
f
Vln. I
p
Vln. II
p
Vla.
Vc.
Db.
p

169
Vln. I
Vln. II
Vla.
Vc.
Db.

172
Vln. I
Vln. II
Vla.
Vc.
Db.

175
1.
Fl.
p
Vln. I
Vln. II
Vla.
Vc.
Db.

178
Adagio
Vln. I
Vln. II
Vla.
Vc.
Db.
p

Tempo I°
180
Fl.
Ob.
Cl.
Bsn.
Hn.
Tpt.
Ten. Tbn. 1.
Ten. Tbn. 2.
Bass Tbn.
Timp.
Tempo I°
Vln. I
Vln. II
Vla.
Vc.
Db.
f
2.

185
Fl.
Ob.
Cl.
Bsn.
a2
Hn.
Tpt.
1.
Ten. Tbn. 1.
Ten. Tbn. 2.
Bass Tbn.
Timp.
Vln. I
Vln. II
Vla.
Vc.
Db.

189
Fl.
Ob.
Cl.
Bsn.
Hn.
Tpt.
Ten. Tbn. 1.
Ten. Tbn. 2.
Bass Tbn.
Timp.
Vln. I
Vln. II
Vla.
Vc.
Db.

194
Fl.
Ob.
Cl.
Bsn.
Hn.
Tpt.
2.
f
Ten. Tbn. 1.
Ten. Tbn. 2.
Bass Tbn.
Timp.
Vln. I
Vln. II
Vla.
Vc.
Db.

199
Fl.
Ob.
Cl.
Bsn.
Hn.
Tpt.
Ten. Tbn. 1.
Ten. Tbn. 2.
Bass Tbn.
Timp.
Vln. I
Vln. II
Vla.
Vc.
Db.
2.
f
sf

202
Fl.
Ob.
Cl.
Bsn.
Hn.
Tpt.
Ten. Tbn. 1.
Ten. Tbn. 2.
Bass Tbn.
Timp.
Vln. I
Vln. II
Vla.
Vc.
Db.
sf

206
Fl.
Ob.
Cl.
Bsn.
Hn.
Tpt.
Ten. Tbn. 1.
Ten. Tbn. 2.
Bass Tbn.
Timp.
Vln. I
Vln. II
Vla.
Vc.
Db.

212
solo
Fl.
Cl.
1.
Bsn.
Vln. I
Vln. II
Vla.
Vc.
Db.
218
Fl.
Bsn.
Vln. I
Vln. II
Vla.
Vc.
Db.

224
Fl.
Bsn.
Hn.
Vln. I
Vln. II
Vla.
Vc.
Db.
p
230
Fl.
Bsn.
Hn.
Vln. I
Vln. II
Vla.
Vc.
Db.

236
Fl.
Ob.
1.
Cl.
Bsn.
a2
Hn.
Tpt.
Ten. Tbn. 1.
Ten. Tbn. 2.
Bass Tbn.
Timp.
Vln. I
Vln. II
Vla.
Vc.
Db.

241
Fl.
(1)
Ob.
(1)
Cl.
Bsn.
Hn.
Tpt.
Ten. Tbn. 1.
Ten. Tbn. 2.
Bass Tbn.
Timp.
Vln. I
Vln. II
Vla.
Vc.
Db.

246
Fl.
Ob.
Cl.
Bsn.
Hn.
Tpt.
Ten. Tbn. 1.
Ten. Tbn. 2.
Bass Tbn.
Timp.
Vln. I
Vln. II
Vla.
Vc.
Db.

250
Fl.
Ob.
Cl.
Bsn.
a2
Hn.
Tpt.
2.
Ten. Tbn. 1.
Ten. Tbn. 2.
Bass Tbn.
Timp.
Vln. I
Vln. II
Vla.
Vc.
Db.

255
(attacca)
Fl.
Ob.
Cl.
Bsn.
a2
Hn.
a2
Tpt.
Ten. Tbn. 1.
Ten. Tbn. 2.
Bass Tbn.
Timp.
(attacca)
Vln. I
Vln. II
Vla.
Vc.
Db.

260
Proserpina:
Halte! Halt einmal,
Unselige! Vergebens
Irrst du in diesen rauhen
Wüsten hin und her!
Stop! Stop, you poor wretch!
In vain you wander
Here and there
in these inclement wastes!
Endlos liegen vor dir
die Trauergefilde und was du suchst,
Endless the fields of sorrow
lie before you and what you seek
Pros.
A
(quasi recit.)
Vln. I
Vln. II
Vla.
Vc.
Db
Vcl
262
Adagio
Allegro
Fl.
Cl.
liegt immer hinter dir.
forever lies behind you.
Tutti

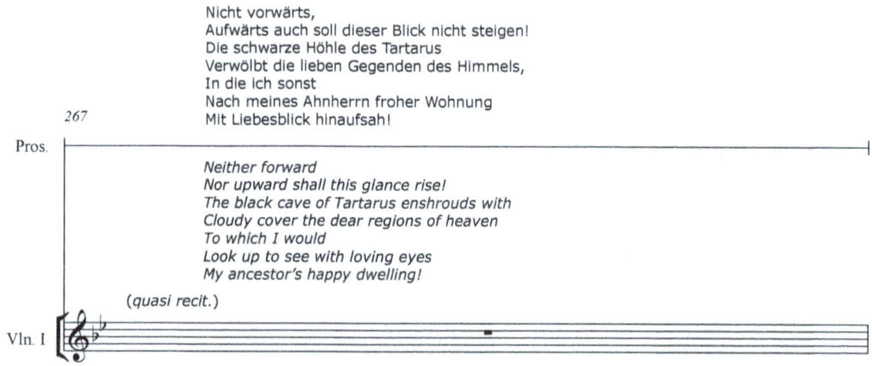
Nicht vorwärts,
Aufwärts auch soll dieser Blick nicht steigen!
Die schwarze Höhle des Tartarus
Verwölbt die lieben Gegenden des Himmels,
In die ich sonst
Nach meines Ahnherrn froher Wohnung
Mit Liebesblick hinaufsah!
267
Pros.
Neither forward
Nor upward shall this glance rise!
The black cave of Tartarus enshrouds with
Cloudy cover the dear regions of heaven
To which I would
Look up to see with loving eyes
My ancestor's happy dwelling!
(quasi recit.)
Vln. I

268
Pros.
Ach! Tochter du des Jupiters, wie tief bist du verloren! –
Alas, daughter of Jupiter, how deeply you are lost!
Vln. I
Vln. II
Vla.
Vc.
Db.
pizz.
pp

B
272 Andante
1.solo
Ob.
Bsn.
1.
Hn.
Andante
arco
Vln. I
arco
Vln. II
arco
Vla.
Vc. arco
Vc.
Db.
Db. arco

278
Ob.
Bsn.
Hn.
Vln. I
Vln. II
Vla.
Vc.
Db.
p
p
p

284
Ob.
Bsn.
Hn.
Vln. I
Vln. II
Vla.
Vc.
Db.
1.
p

Gespielinnen!
Als jene blumenreiche Täler
Für uns gesamt noch blühten,
Als an dem himmelklaren Strom des Alpheus
Wir plätschernd noch im Abendstrahle scherzten,
Einander Kränze wanden
Und heimlich an den Jüngling dachten,
Dessen Haupt unser Herz sie widmete,
Da war uns keine Nacht zu tief zum Schwätzen,
Keine Zeit zu lang,
Um freundliche Geschichten zu wiederholen,
Und die Sonne
Riß leichter nicht aus ihrem Silberbette
Sich auf, als wir, voll Lust zu leben,
Früh im Tau die Rosenfüße badeten.

Pros.

Playmates!
When those valleys, rich in flowers,
Still blossomed for us all,
When we splashed and laughed in the evening
Sun by the heavenly clear stream of Alpheus,
Wove garlands for each other,
And secretly recalled the youth
To whom our heart dedicated them:
Then no night was too deep for our conversation,
No hour too long
For the retelling of friendly stories,
And the sun
Did not rise more easily out of its silver bed
Than we returned early, full of joy for life,
To bathe our rosy feet in the dew.

un poco più Allegro
291
Ob.
Bsn.
un poco più Allegro
Vln. I
Vln. II
Vla.
Vc.
Db.
296
Bsn.
O Mädchen! Mädchen!
Die ihr, einsam nun,
Zerstreut an jenen Quellen schleicht,
Die Blumen auflest,
Die ich, ach, Entführte!
Aus meinem Schoße fallen ließ,
Ihr steht und seht mir nach,
wohin ich verschwand
Pros.
O maidens, maidens!
Who wander alone,
Absent-minded by those streams,
Gathering the flowers
That I, alas, the abducted,
Let fall from my lap,
You stop to look for me,
To see whither I disappeared.
Vln. I
Vln. II
Vla.
Vc.
Db.

C
298
Allegro assai
Fl.
Ob.
Cl.
Bsn.
Pros.
C
Allegro assai
Vln. I
Vln. II
Vla.
Vc.
Db.

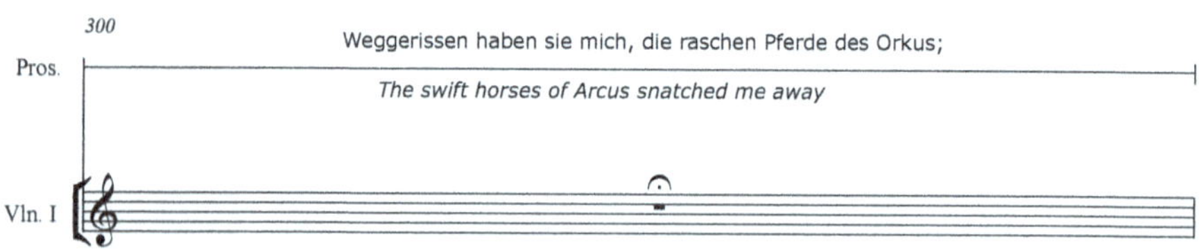
300
Pros.
Weggerissen haben sie mich, die raschen Pferde des Orkus;
The swift horses of Arcus snatched me away
Vln. I

301
Fl.
Ob.
Cl.
Bsn.
Hn.
Pros.
Mit festen Armen
Hielt mich der unerbittliche Gott!
With firm arms
The merciless God held me tight!
Vln. I
Vln. II
Vla.
Vc.
Db.

304
Fl.
Ob.
Bsn.
Hn.
Pros.
Vln. I
Vln. II
Vla.
Vc.
Db.
308
Pros.
Amor! ach Amor! Floh lachend auf zum Olymp!
Amor, O Amor! Fled laughing up to Olympus!
Vln. I

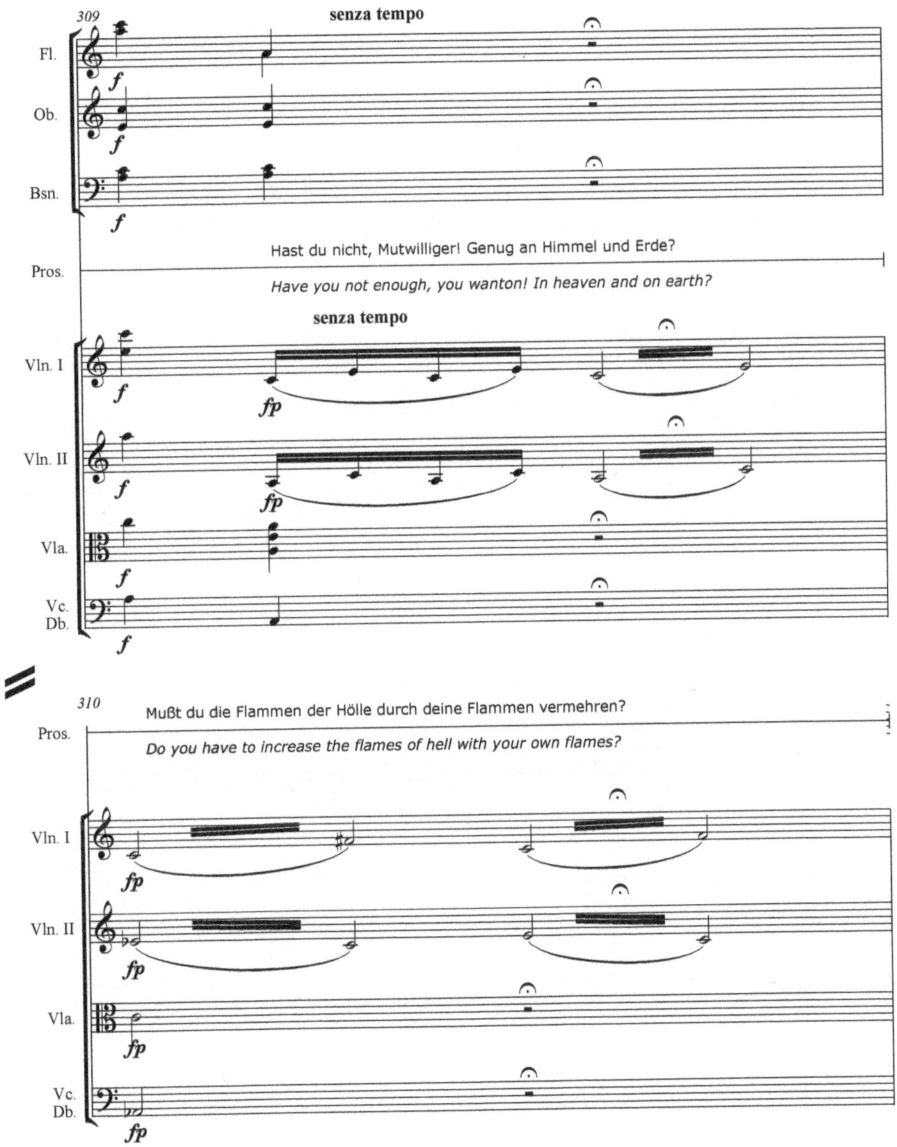
309
senza tempo
Fl.
Ob.
Bsn.
Pros.
Hast du nicht, Mutwilliger! Genug an Himmel und Erde?
Have you not enough, you wanton! In heaven and on earth?
senza tempo
Vln. I
Vln. II
Vla.
Vc.
Db.
310
Pros.
Mußt du die Flammen der Hölle durch deine Flammen vermehren?
Do you have to increase the flames of hell with your own flames?
Vln. I
Vln. II
Vla.
Vc.
Db.

311
Allegro assai
Fl.
Ob.
Cl.
Bsn.
Hn.
Tpts.
Timp.
Pros.
Allegro assai
Vln. I
Vln. II
Vla.
Vc.
Db.

314
senza tempo
Fl.
Ob.
Cl.
Bsn.
Tpts.
Timp.
Pros.
Heruntergerissen in diese endlosen Tiefen!
Snatched down into these endless depths!
senza tempo
Vln. I
Vln. II
Vla.
Vc.
Db.

316
Fl.
Ob.
Cl.
Bsn.
Tpts.
Timp.
Pros.
Königin hier!
To be Queen here!
Königin?
Queen?
Vor der nur Schatten sich neigen!
Before whom only shades will bow!
Vln. I
Vln. II
Vla.
Vc.
Db.

D
319
Allegro sostenuto
Fl.
Ob.
Cl.
Bsn.
Hn.
Tpts.
Tbn. 1
Tbn. 2
Bass Tbn.
Timp.
Pros.
D Allegro sostenuto
Vln. I
Vln. II
Vla.
Vc.
Db.

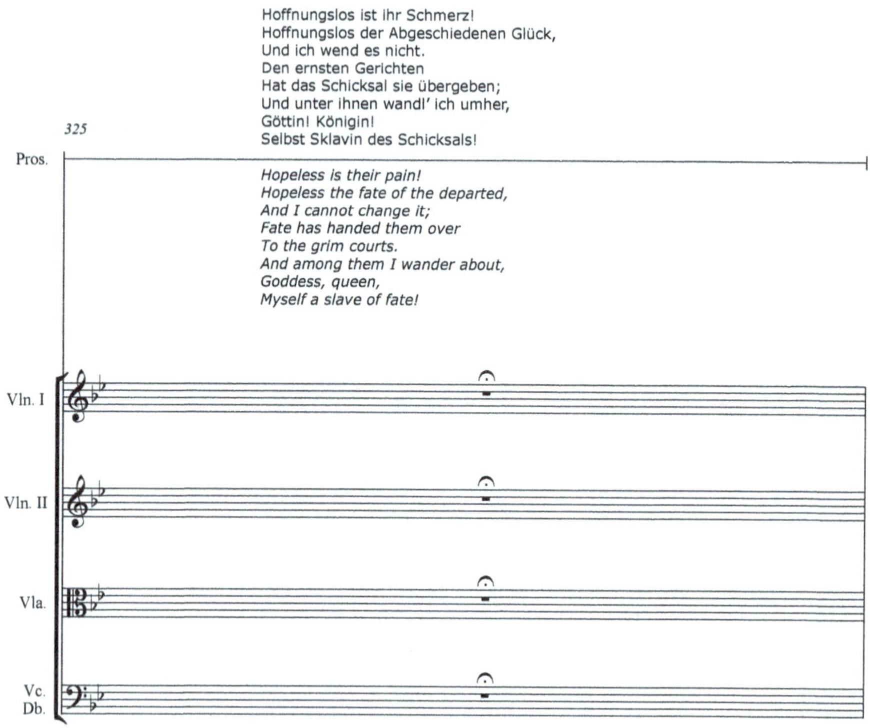
Hoffnungslos ist ihr Schmerz!
Hoffnungslos der Abgeschiedenen Glück,
Und ich wend es nicht.
Den ernsten Gerichten
Hat das Schicksal sie übergeben;
Und unter ihnen wandl' ich umher,
Göttin! Königin!
Selbst Sklavin des Schicksals!
325
Pros.
Hopeless is their pain!
Hopeless the fate of the departed,
And I cannot change it;
Fate has handed them over
To the grim courts.
And among them I wander about,
Goddess, queen,
Myself a slave of fate!
Vln. I
Vln. II
Vla.
Vc.
Db.

326
[Allegro sostenuto]
Fl.
Ob.
Cl.
Bsn.
Hn.
Tpts.
Tbn. 1
Tbn. 2
Bass Tbn.
Timp.
[Allegro sostenuto]
Vln. I
Vln. II
Vla.
Vcl.
Vc.
Db.

333 Ach, das fliehende Wasser
Möcht ich dem Tantalus schöpfen,

Mit lieblichen Früchten ihn sättigen!
Armer Alter!
Für gereiztes Verlangen gestraft!

Pros.

Oh, I would like to draw the fleeing water
For Tantalus!

Satisfy him with sweet fruits!
Poor old man,
Punished for provoked craving!

337 In Ixions Rad möcht ich greifen,
Einhalten seinen Schmerz!

Aber was vermögen wir Götter
Über die ewigen Qualen!

Pros.

I would like to stop Ixion's wheel
And put an end to his pain!

But what can we gods do
Against eternal punishment!

* This section down to figure E is basically Andante, apart from bars 337-38. The couplet 'In Ixions Rad möcht ich greifen, /Einhalten seinen Schmerz' must coincide with these two *Allegro* bars. Otherwise a certain liberty can be taken with the placing of the text in order to allow the meaning and the significance of the words to come across in performance.

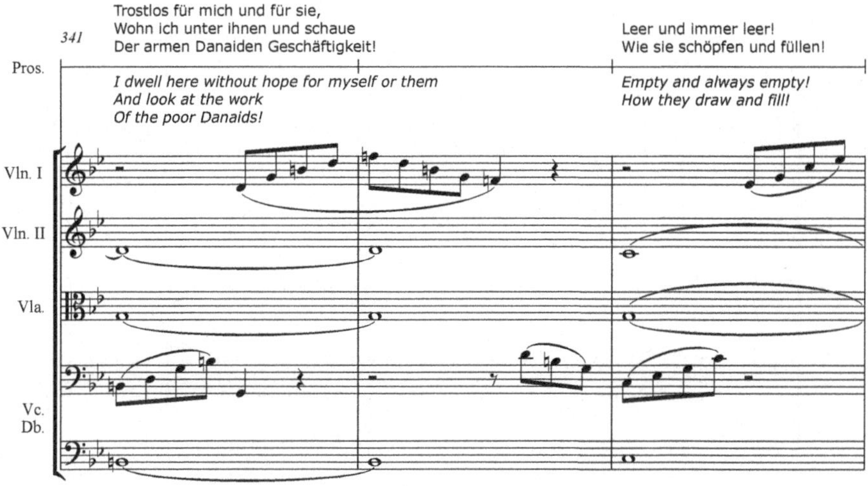
341
Trostlos für mich und für sie,
Wohn ich unter ihnen und schaue
Der armen Danaiden Geschäftigkeit!
Leer und immer leer!
Wie sie schöpfen und füllen!
Pros.
I dwell here without hope for myself or them
And look at the work
Of the poor Danaids!
Empty and always empty!
How they draw and fill!
Vln. I
Vln. II
Vla.
Vc.
Db.

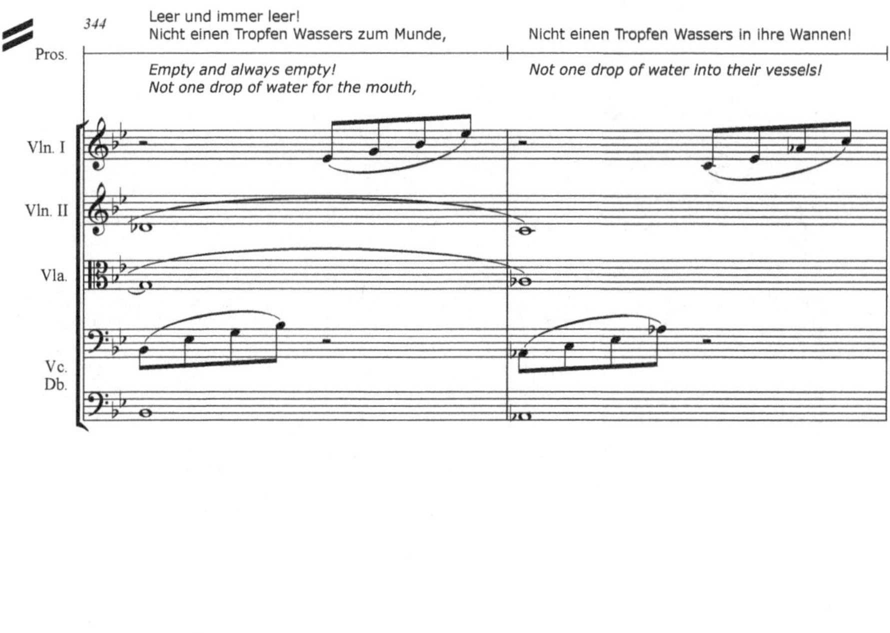
344
Leer und immer leer!
Nicht einen Tropfen Wassers zum Munde,
Nicht einen Tropfen Wassers in ihre Wannen!
Pros.
Empty and always empty!
Not one drop of water for the mouth,
Not one drop of water into their vessels!
Vln. I
Vln. II
Vla.
Vc.
Db.

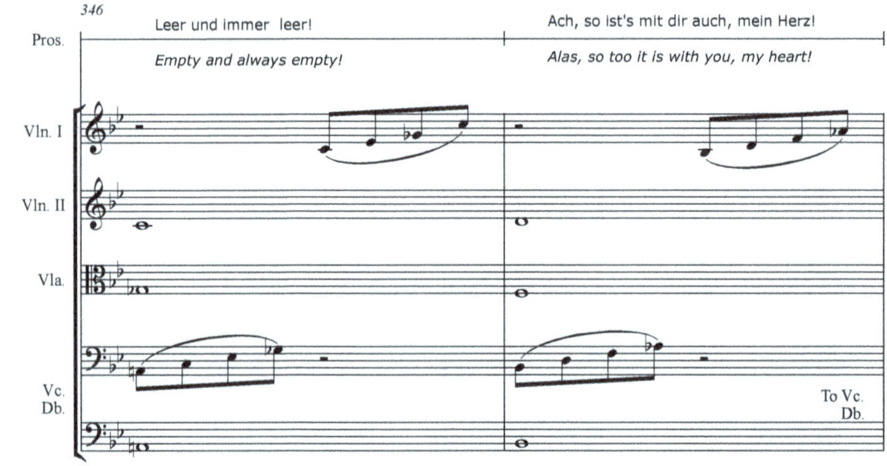
346
Pros.
Leer und immer leer!
Empty and always empty!
Ach, so ist's mit dir auch, mein Herz!
Alas, so too it is with you, my heart!
Vln. I
Vln. II
Vla.
Vc.
Db.
To Vc.
Db.

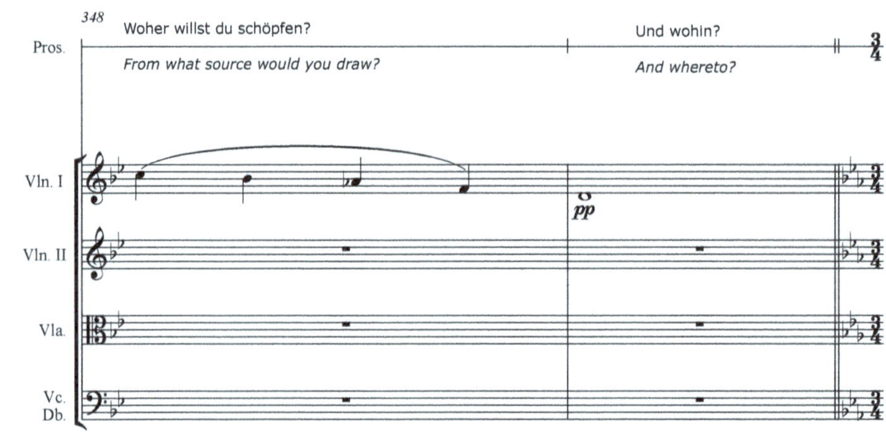
348
Pros.
Woher willst du schöpfen?
From what source would you draw?
Und wohin?
And whereto?
Vln. I
pp
Vln. II
Vla.
Vc.
Db.

358

Pros.

Euer ruhiges Wandeln, Selige,
Streicht nur vor mir vorüber;
Mein Weg ist nicht mit euch!

Your quiet strolling, dead and departed,
Passes me by;
My way is not with you!

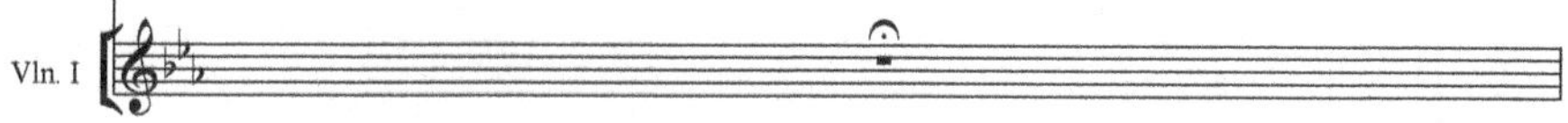

Pros.

In euren leichten Tänzen,

In your playful dances,

In euren tiefen Hainen,

In your deep groves,

362
Bsn.
Hns.
In eurer lispelnden Wohnung
Pros.
In your whispering dwelling
365
Bsn.
Hns.
Rauscht's nicht von Leben wie droben,
Schwankt nicht von Schmerz zu Lust
Pros.
The teeming sounds of life are silent;
There is no vascillation from grief
367
Bsn.
Hns.
Der Seligkeit Fülle.
Pros.
To full bliss.
tutti
Vln. I
tutti
Vln. II
tutti
Vla.
tutti
Vc.
Db.

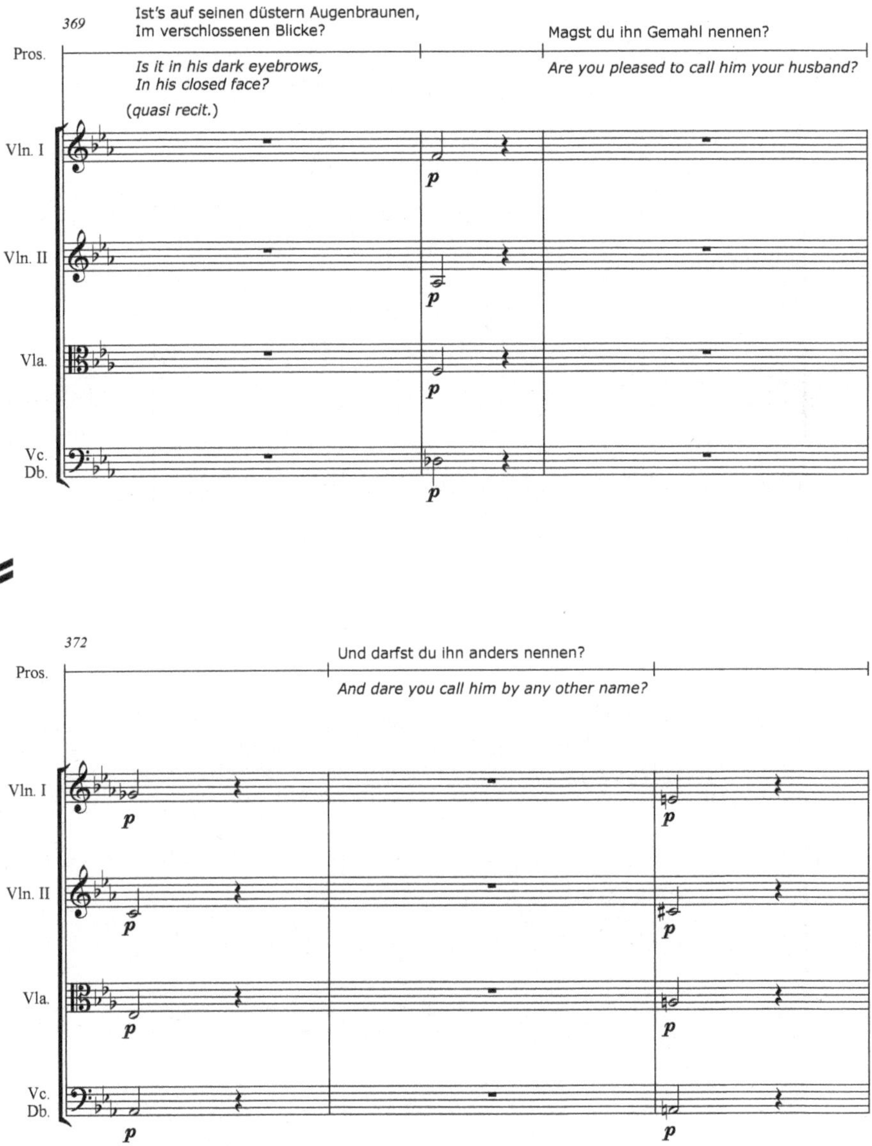
369
Ist's auf seinen düstern Augenbraunen,
Im verschlossenen Blicke?
Magst du ihn Gemahl nennen?
Pros.
Is it in his dark eyebrows,
In his closed face?
Are you pleased to call him your husband?
(quasi recit.)
Vln. I
Vln. II
Vla.
Vc.
Db.
372
Und darfst du ihn anders nennen?
And dare you call him by any other name?

375
Pros.
Liebe! Liebe!
Warum öffnetest du sein Herz
Auf einen Augenblick?
Love! Love!
Why did you open his heart
For a moment?
Und warum nach mir?
Da du wußtest,
Es werde sich wieder
auf ewig verschließen?
And why to me?
Since you knew
That it would close again
forever?
Vln. I
Vln. II
Vla.
Vc.
Db.
p

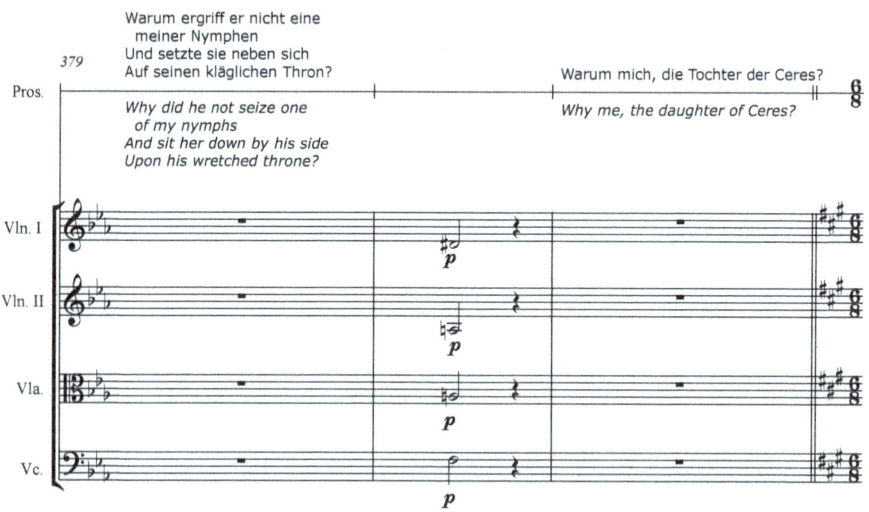
379
Pros.
Warum ergriff er nicht eine
meiner Nymphen
Und setzte sie neben sich
Auf seinen kläglichen Thron?
Why did he not seize one
of my nymphs
And sit her down by his side
Upon his wretched throne?
Warum mich, die Tochter der Ceres?
Why me, the daughter of Ceres?
Vln. I
Vln. II
Vla.
Vc.
p

F
Andante
Clarinet in A*
solo
382
Cl.
Vln. I
Vln. II
Vla.
Vc.
Vcl
pizz.
sf
p
*suoni reali

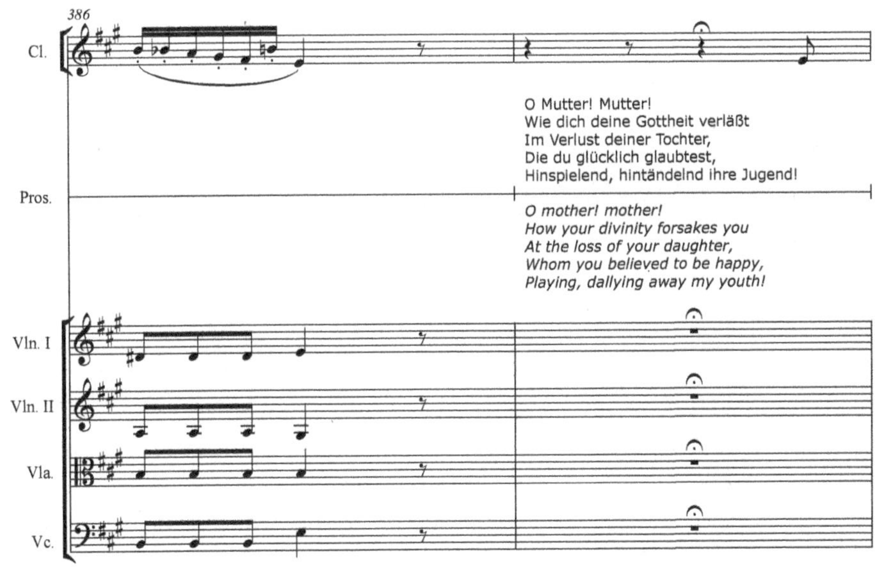
386
Cl.
O Mutter! Mutter!
Wie dich deine Gottheit verläßt
Im Verlust deiner Tochter,
Die du glücklich glaubtest,
Hinspielend, hintändelnd ihre Jugend!
Pros.
O mother! mother!
How your divinity forsakes you
At the loss of your daughter,
Whom you believed to be happy,
Playing, dallying away my youth!
Vln. I
Vln. II
Vla.
Vc.

388
Cl.
Vln. I
Vln. II
Vla.
Vc.
arco
arco
arco
arco
p
p
p
p

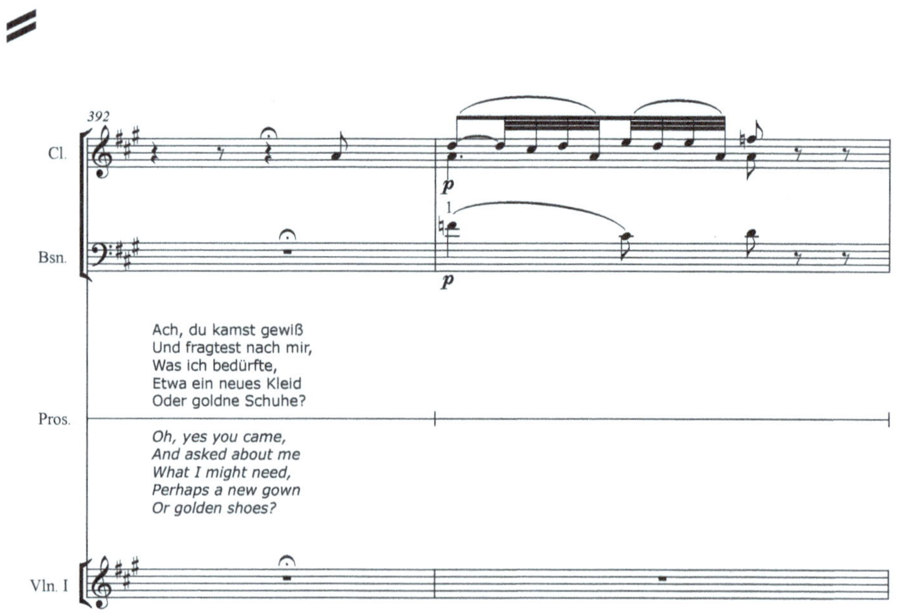
392
Cl.
Bsn.
Pros.
Vln. I
p
p
Ach, du kamst gewiß
Und fragtest nach mir,
Was ich bedürfte,
Etwa ein neues Kleid
Oder goldne Schuhe?
Oh, yes you came,
And asked about me
What I might need,
Perhaps a new gown
Or golden shoes?

394
senza tempo
Cl.
Bsn.
p
p
Und du fandest die Mädchen
An ihre Weiden gefesselt,
Wo sie mich verloren,
Nicht wieder fanden,
Ihre Locken zerrauften,
Erbärmlich klagten,
Pros.
And you found the maidens
Tied to their willows,
Where they lost me
And did not find me,
Tearing their hair out,
Lamenting pitifully,
Vln. I

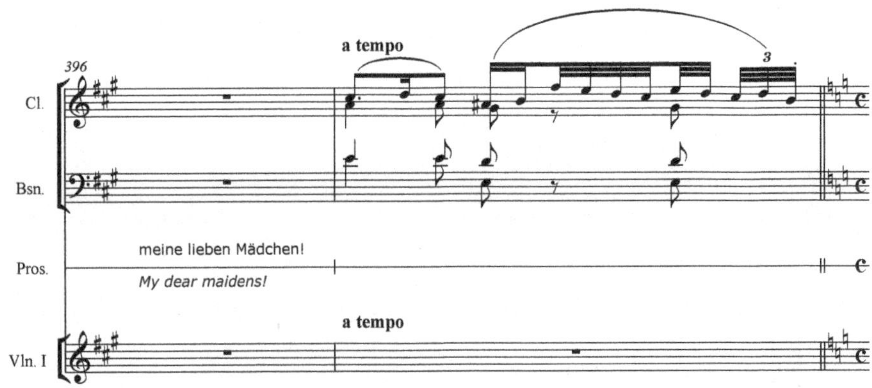
396
a tempo
Cl.
Bsn.
meine lieben Mädchen!
Pros.
My dear maidens!
a tempo
Vln. I

G
Allegro vivace
398
(quasi recit.)
Cl.
Bsn.
Pros.
'Wohin ist sie? Wohin?', rufst du.
'Where has she gone? Where?', you cry.
Allegro vivace
(quasi recit.)
Vln. I
ff
Vln. II
ff
Vla.
ff
Tutti
Vc.
ff

400
Pros.
'Welchen Weg nahm der Verruchte?
'What path did the scoundrel take?
Soll er ungestraft Jupiters Stamm entweihen?
Shall he, unpunished, desecrate Jupiter's line?
Vln. I
ff
Vln. II
ff
Vla.
ff
Vc.
ff

402
Wohin geht der
Pfad seiner Rosse?
Pros.
Where does the trail
of his horses lead?
Vln. I
Vln. II
Vla.
Vc.
404
Fackeln her!
Durch die Nacht
will ich ihn verfolgen!
Will keine Stunde ruhen,
bis ich sie finde,
Pros.
Torches here!
In the night
I will pursue him!
I will not rest a single hour
until I find her,
Vln. I
Vln. II
Vla.
Vc.
406
Will keinen Gang scheuen
Hierhin und dorthin!'
Pros.
I will eschew no path
Here or there!'
Vln. I
Vln. II
Vla.
Vc.

H
Presto
408
Fl.
Ob.
Clarinet in B♭ *
Cl.
Bsn.
a2
Hns.
Tpts.
Tbn. 1
Tbn. 2
Bass Tbn.
muta in D & A
Timp.
Pros.
H
Presto
Vln. I
Vln. II
Vla.
Vc.
cresc.
p cresc.
mf cresc.
*suoni reali

412
(quasi recit.)
Fl.
Ob.
Cl.
Bsn.
Hns.
Tpts.
Tbn. 1
Tbn. 2
Bass Tbn.
Timp.
Pros.
Dir blinken deine Drachen mit klugen Augen zu,
Aller Pfade gewohnt, folgen sie deinem Lenken:
Your dragons look at you with knowing eyes;
Accustomed to all paths, they follow your lead:
In der unbewohnten
Wüste treibt dich's irre —
You are driven astray
in uninhabited deserts —
(quasi recit.)
Vln. I
Vln. II
Vla.
Vc.

414
[Presto]
Vln. I
Vln. II
Vla.
Vc.
p
p
p
p
p
p

417
Vln. I
Vln. II
Vla.
Vc.
p

420
Fl.
f
Ob.
f
Cl.
Bsn.
f
Hns.
Tpts.
Tbn. 1
Tbn. 2
Bass Tbn.
f
Timp.
Pros.
Vln. I
f
Vln. II
f
Vla.
f
Vc.
f

423

Ach, nur hierher, hierher nicht!
Nicht in die Tiefe der Nacht,
Unbetreten den Ewiglebenden,
Wo, bedeckt von beschwerendem Graus,
Deine Tochter ermattet!

Pros.

Oh, only not here, not here
Not into the depths of the night.
Untrodden by the eternal gods, where,
Overburdened by the horror,
Your daughter languishes!

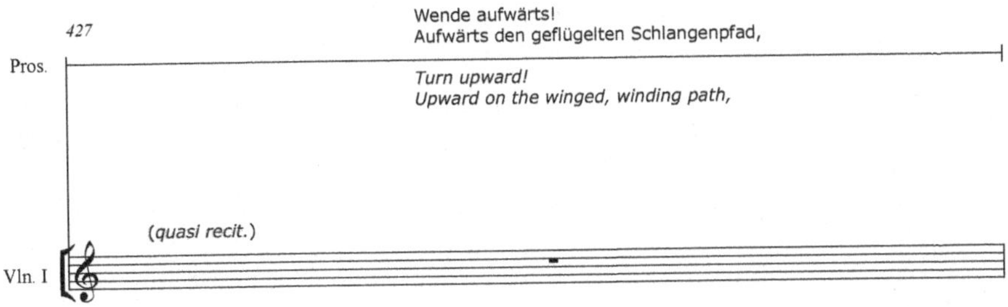
427
Wende aufwärts!
Aufwärts den geflügelten Schlangenpfad,
Pros.
Turn upward!
Upward on the winged, winding path,
(quasi recit.)
Vln. I

428
Aufwärts nach Jupiters Wohnung!
Pros.
Upward to Jupiter's dwelling!
Vln. I
Vln. II
Vla.
Vc.

431
Der weiß es, der allein, der Erhabene,
Wo deine Tochter ist!
He knows it, the great god, he alone knows
Where your daughter is.
Pros.
Vln. I
Vln. II
Vla.
Vc.

I
Larghetto
433
Vla.
Vc.
Vc.
Db
solo

436

Pros.

Vater der Götter und Menschen!
Ruhst du noch oben auf deinem goldenen Stuhle,
Zu dem du mich Kleine
So oft mit Freundlichkeit aufhobst,
In deinen Händen mich scherzend
Gegen den endlosen Himmel schwenktest,
Daß ich kindisch droben zu verschweben bebte?
Bist du's noch, Vater? –

Father of gods and men!
Do you sit even now above on your golden throne
To which you so often raised me up
When I was little, laughing and lovingly
Swinging me in your arms
Toward the infinite sky, so that I, child that I was
Feared to stay hovering up there?
Are you still there, father?

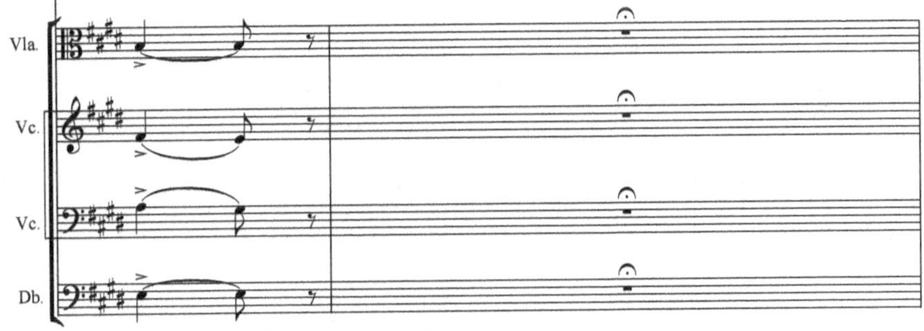

438

Pros.

Nicht zu deinem Haupte
In dem ewigen Blau
Des feuerdurchwebten Himmels,
Hier! Hier! –

Not to you
In the eternal blue skies
Lit up with fire,
But here, here!

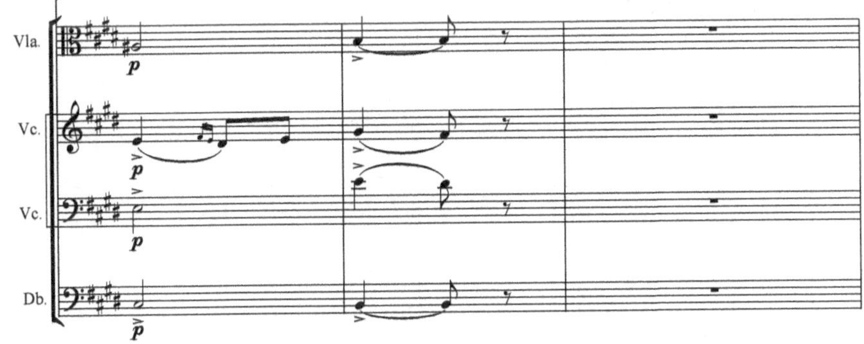

444

Pros.

Leite sie her!
Daß ich auf mit ihr
Aus diesem Kerker fahre!
Daß mir Phöbus wieder
Seine lieben Strahlen bringe,
Luna wieder
Aus den Silberlocken lächle!

Guide her here,
That I may ride up with her
Out of this dungeon!
That Phoebus may bring me
His lovely rays once more,
That Luna may smile at me again
From her silvery tresses!

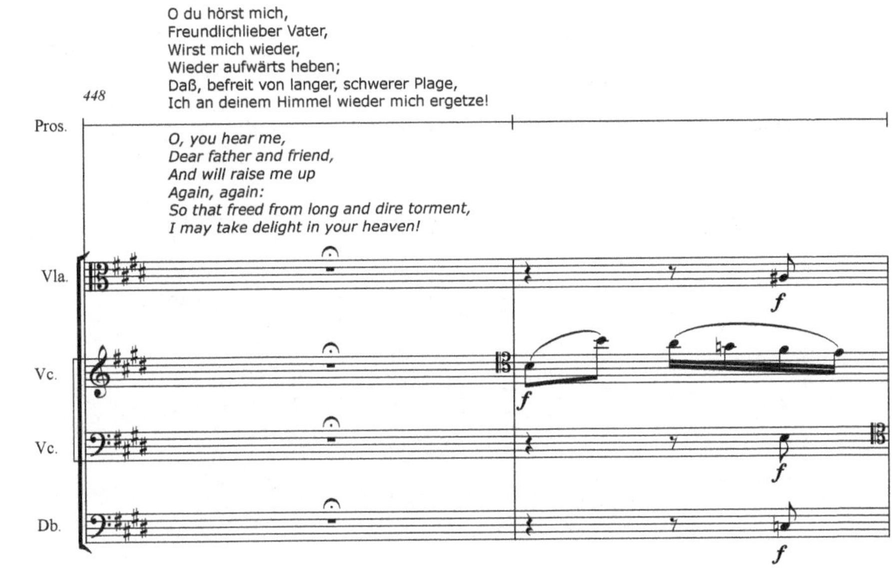
448
Pros.
O du hörst mich,
Freundlichlieber Vater,
Wirst mich wieder,
Wieder aufwärts heben;
Daß, befreit von langer, schwerer Plage,
Ich an deinem Himmel wieder mich ergetze!
O, you hear me,
Dear father and friend,
And will raise me up
Again, again:
So that freed from long and dire torment,
I may take delight in your heaven!
Vla.
Vc.
Vc.
Db.

450
Pros.
Letze dich, verzagtes Herz!
Ach! Hoffnung!
Hoffnung gießt
In Sturmnacht Morgenröte!
Be refreshed, despondent heart!
Oh! Hope!
Hope pours the sunrise
Into the stormy night!
Vla.
a piacere
Vc.
a piacere
Vc.
Db.

452
Allegretto
tutti
Vln. I
Vln. II
Vla.
Vc.
Vc.
Db.
p
sfz
f
pp
456
Pros.
Dieser Boden ist nicht Fels,
Nicht Moos mehr;
This ground is not rock,
No longer moss,
Diese Berge
Nicht voll schwarzen Grauses!
These mountains
Are not full of black horror!
Vln. I
Vln. II
Vla.
Vc.
Db.
pp

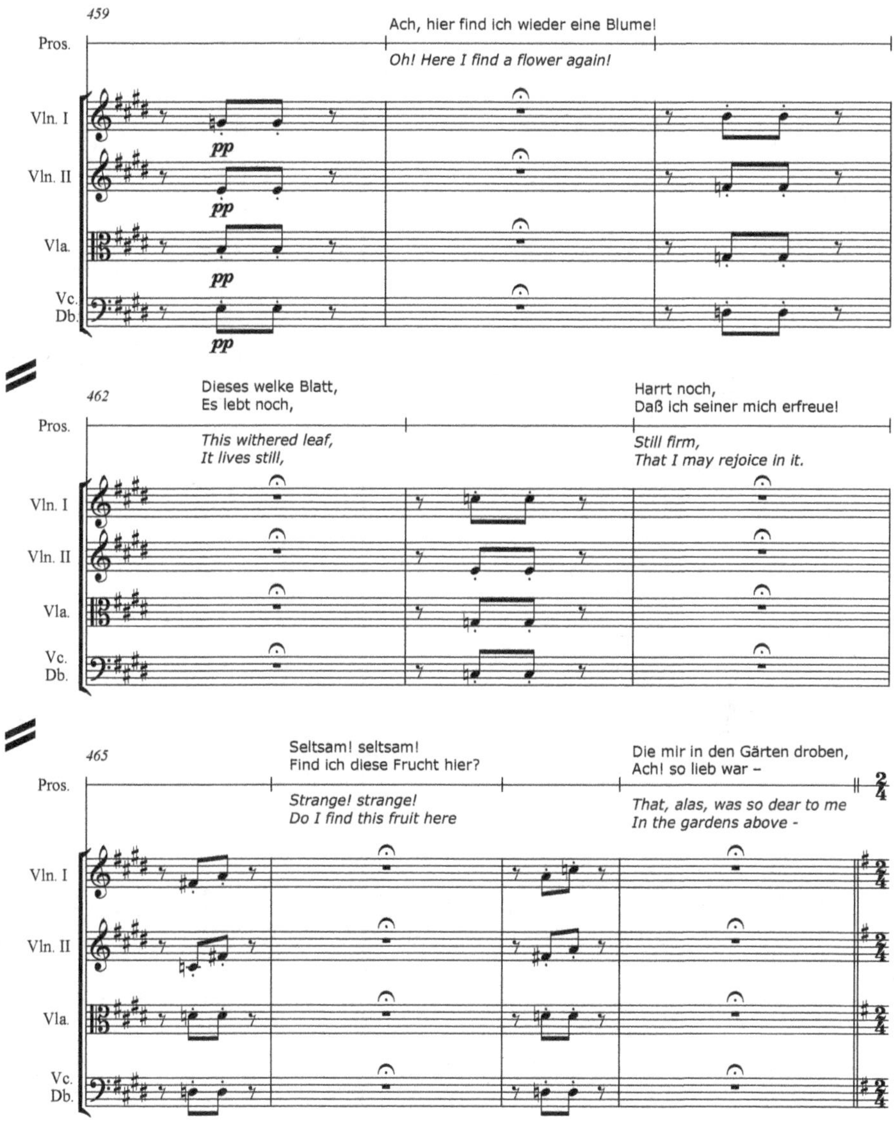
459
Pros.
Ach, hier find ich wieder eine Blume!
Oh! Here I find a flower again!
Vln. I
Vln. II
Vla.
Vc.
Db.
pp
462
Dieses welke Blatt,
Es lebt noch,
This withered leaf,
It lives still,
Harrt noch,
Daß ich seiner mich erfreue!
Still firm,
That I may rejoice in it.
465
Seltsam! seltsam!
Find ich diese Frucht hier?
Strange! strange!
Do I find this fruit here
Die mir in den Gärten droben,
Ach! so lieb war –
That, alas, was so dear to me
In the gardens above -

Andantino quasi Allegretto
J
(Sie bricht den Granatapfel ab.)
(She breaks open the pomegranate)
469
1. solo
Fl.
p
Andantino quasi Allegretto
Vln. I
Vln. II
Vla.

474
Fl.
Vln. I
Vln. II
Vla.

Laß dich genießen,
Freundliche Frucht!
Laß mich vergessen
Alle den Harm!
Wieder mich wähnen
Droben in Jugend,
In der vertaumelten
Lieblichen Zeit,
In den umduftenden
Himmlischen Blüten,
In den Gerüchen
Seliger Wonne,
Die der Entzückten,
Der Schmachtenden ward!

Pros.

Let me savour you,
Friendly fruit!
Let me forget
All my sorrow!
Let me pretend
I am above
In my youth again
The whirl of
Those lovely days,
Amid the fragrant
Heavenly flowers,
Amid the fragrances
Of joyful bliss
That I, ravished and languished,
Once knew!

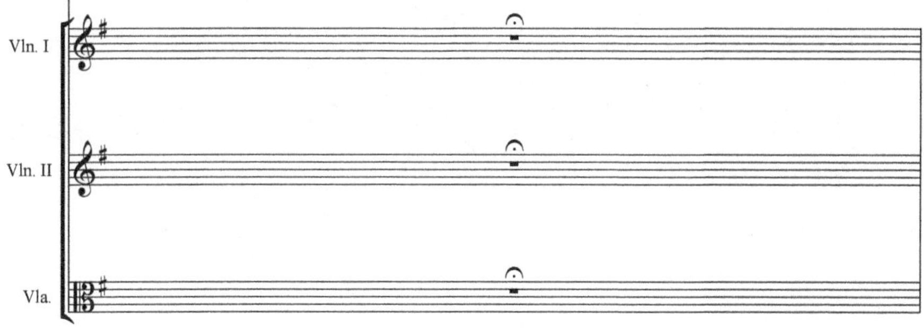

(Sie ißt einige Körner.)
(She eats some seeds.)
479
Fl.
Pros.
Vln. I
Vln. II
Vla.
483
Labend!
Labend!
Refreshing!
Refreshing!

487
Allegro
Fl.
Wie greift's auf einmal
Durch diese Freuden,
Durch diese offne Wonne
Mit entsetzlichen Schmerzen,
Mit eisernen Händen
Der Hölle durch! —
Pros.
But how is it
That abysmal pains
And the iron hands of Hell
Penetrate all at once
through these joys,
Through this open bliss! —
Allegro
Vln. I
Vln. II
Vla.
Vc.
Db

490
(quasi recit.)
Ob.
Bsn.
Pros.
Was hab ich verbrochen,
Daß ich genoß?
What crime have I committed
By enjoying?
(quasi recit.)
Vln. I
Vln. II
Vla.
Vc.
Db
493
Timp.
Pros.
Ach! Warum schafft
Die erste Freude hier mir Qual?
Alas! Why does this first joy
Bring me torment here?
Was ist's?
What is it?
was ist's?
What is it?
Vln. I
Vln. II
Vla.
Vc.
Db

497
Fl.
Ob.
Cl.
Bsn.
Hn.
Tpt.
Ten. Tbn. 1
Ten. Tbn. 2
Bass Tbn.
Timp.
Pros.
Ihr Felsen scheint hier
schrecklicher herabzuwinken,
You cliffs seem to glower
at me more horribly,
Vln. I
Vln. II
Vla.
Vc.
Db

499
Fl.
Ob.
Cl.
Bsn.
Hn.
Tpt.
Ten. Tbn. 1
Ten. Tbn. 2
Bass Tbn.
Timp.
Pros.
Mich fester zu umfassen!
To grip me more tightly!
Vln. I
Vln. II
Vla.
Vc.
Db

501
Fl.
Ob.
Cl.
Bsn.
Hn.
Tpt.
Ten. Tbn. 1
Ten. Tbn. 2
Bass Tbn.
Timp.
tr
p
Pros.
Ihr Wolken tiefer mich zu drücken!
To oppress me further!
Im fernen Schoße des Abgrunds
Dumpfe Gewitter tosend sich zu erzeugen!
In the depths of the abyss,
Muted thunderstorms begin to roll!
Vln. I
Vln. II
Vla.
Vc.
Db
pp
pp
pp
pp

[Allegro]
503
Fl.
Ob.
Cl.
Bsn.
Hn.
Tpt.
Ten. Tbn. 1
Ten. Tbn. 2
Bass Tbn.
Timp.
Pros.
Und ihr weiten Reiche der Parzen
Mir zuzurufen: Du bist unser!
And you vast regions of the Fates
Seem to call to me: You are ours!
[Allegro]
Vln. I
Vln. II
Vla.
Vc.
Db

505
Fl.
Ob.
Cl.
Bsn.
Hn.
a2
Tpt.
Ten. Tbn. 1
Ten. Tbn. 2
Bass Tbn.
Timp.
tr
Vln. I
Vln. II
Vla.
Vc.
Db
ff

DIE PARZEN *(unsichtbar)*
The Fates *(off-stage)*

520
Pros.
Hast du's gesprochen,
You have spoken,
L Allegro
(quasi recit.)
Vln. I
Vln. II
Vla.
Vc.
Db.
522
Vater!
Father!
Warum? warum?
Was tat ich, daß du mich verstößest?
Why? Why?
What did I do for you to cast me out?
523
Warum rufst du mich nicht
Zu deinem lichten Thron auf?
Why do you not call me up
To your radiant throne?
Warum den Apfel?
O verflucht die Früchte!
Why the pomegranate?
O curse the fruits!

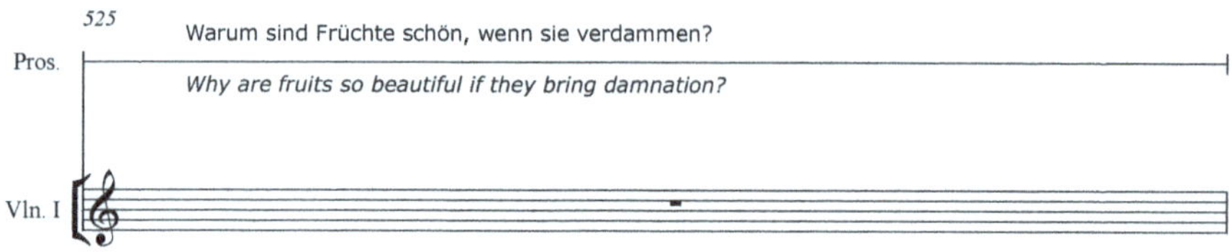
525
Pros.
Warum sind Früchte schön, wenn sie verdammen?
Why are fruits so beautiful if they bring damnation?
Vln. I

526
[Allegro]
Fl.
Ob.
Bsn.
a2
f
[Allegro]
Vln. I
Vln. II
Vla.
Vc.
Db.

M
Adagio
(Orchestra tacet)
CHOIR II
528
S A
T I T II
B
Bist nun un - ser! Wa - rum trau - erst du? Sieh, wir ehr - en dich! Un - sre Kö - ni - gin!
You are ours now! Why do you la - ment? See, we hon - our you! You, our no - ble queen!

533
Pros.
N
Allegro assai
Vln. I
Vln. II
Vla.
Vc. Db.
O wäre der Tartarus nicht eure Wohnung,
Daß ich euch hin verwünschen könnte!
O if only Tartarus were not already your
Dwelling that I could banish you there!

536
Pros.
O wäre der Cocyt nicht euer ewig Bad,
Daß ich für euch
Noch Flammen übrig hätte!
O if only Cocytus were not already your eternal bath
so that I might have
Flames left over for you!
Vln. I
Vln. II
Vla.
Vc.
Db.

539
Pros.
Ich, Königin,
Und kann euch nicht vernichten!
I am the queen
And I cannot annihilate you!
Vln. I
Vln. II
Vla.
Vc.
Db.

542
Fl.
Ob.
Cl.
Bsn.
Hn.
Tpt.
Ten. Tbn. 1
Ten. Tbn. 2
Bass Tbn.
Timp.
Pros.
Vln. I
Vln. II
Vla.
Vc.
Db.
In ewigem Haß sei ich mit euch verbunden! —
May I be bound to you in eternal hatred! —

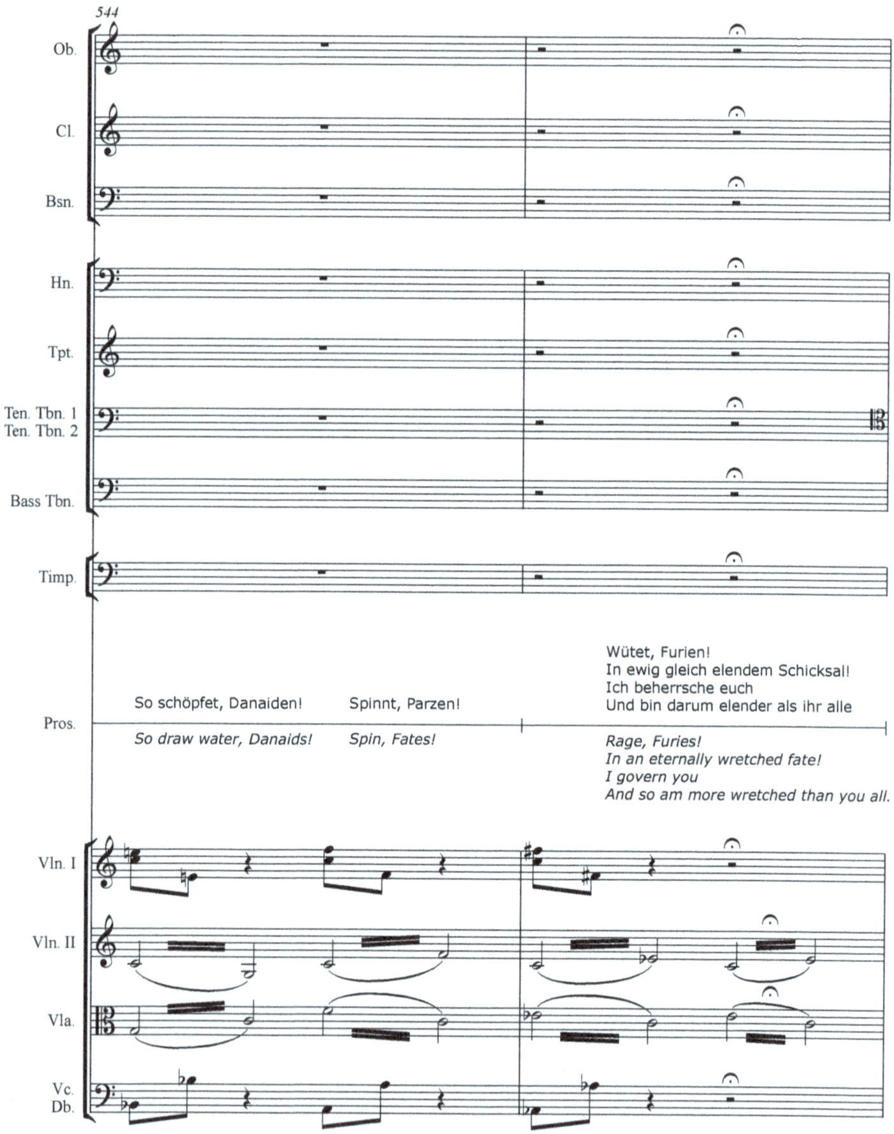
544
Ob.
Cl.
Bsn.
Hn.
Tpt.
Ten. Tbn. 1
Ten. Tbn. 2
Bass Tbn.
Timp.
Pros.
So schöpfet, Danaiden!
So draw water, Danaids!
Spinnt, Parzen!
Spin, Fates!
Wütet, Furien!
In ewig gleich elendem Schicksal!
Ich beherrsche euch
Und bin darum elender als ihr alle
Rage, Furies!
In an eternally wretched fate!
I govern you
And so am more wretched than you all.
Vln. I
Vln. II
Vla.
Vc.
Db.

546
[Allegro assai]
Fl.
Ob.
Cl.
Bsn.
a2
Hn.
Tpt.
Ten. Tbn. 1
Ten. Tbn. 2
Bass Tbn.
Timp.
Pros.
[Allegro assai]
Vln. I
Vln. II
Vla.
Vc.
Db.

550
O
Adagio
Ob.
Cl.
Bsn.
Hn.
Tpt.
Ten. Tbn. 1
Ten. Tbn. 2
Bass Tbn.
Timp.
CHOIR I
S A
T
B B
CHOIR II
S A
T T
B B
Du bist un - ser!
You are ours now!
Wir nei - gen uns dir!
We bow to you!
O
Adagio
Vc.
Db.

554
Ob.
Cl.
Bsn.
Hn.
Tpt.
Ten. Tbn. 1
Ten. Tbn. 2
Bass Tbn.
Timp.
2.
a2
unis.
Bist__ un - ser! Un - ser! Ho - he Kö - ni - gin!
You are ours now! Ours now! You, our no - ble queen!
Vc.
Db.

559
P
Allegro assai
Fl.
Ob.
Bsn.
Pros.
Fern! weg von mir
Sei eure Treu und Herrlichkeit!
Away, away from me
with your fidelity and your glory!
P
Allegro assai
Vln. I
Vln. II
Vla.
Vc.
Db.
562
Pros.
Wie haß ich euch!
Und dich, wie zehnfach haß ich dich
How I hate you!
And you, how I hate you tenfold,
Vln. I
Vln. II
Vla.
Vc.
Db.

564
Weh mir! Ich fühle schon
Die verhaßten Umarmungen
Pros.
Woe is me! I already feel
The abhorrent embraces.
Vln. I
Vln. II
Vla.
Vcl
Tutti
Vc.
Db.
567
Ten. Tbn.
Bass Tbn.
Choirs I & II
(in unison)
S
A
Un - ser! Un - - sre Kön - i - gin!
Ours now! You our no - ble queen!
T
T
Un - ser! Un - - sre Kön - i - gin!
Ours now! You our no - ble queen!
B
B
Un - ser! Un - - sre Kön - i - gin!
Ours now! You our no - ble queen!
Pros.
Vln. I
Vln. II
Vla.
Vc.
Db.

570
Fl.
Ob.
Cl.
Bsn.
a2
Hn.
Tpt.
Ten. Tbn. 1
Ten. Tbn. 2
Bass Tbn.
Timp.
tr
Vln. I
Vln. II
Vla.
Vc.
Db.
f

572
Ob.
Cl.
Bsn.
Hn.
Tpt.
Ten. Tbn. 1
Ten. Tbn. 2
Bass Tbn.
Timp.
Warum reckst du sie nach mir?
Recke sie nach dem Avernus!
Pros.
Why do you stretch out your arms to me?
Stretch them out to Avernus!
Vln. I
Vln. II
Vla.
Vc.
Db.

574
Ob.
Cl.
Bsn.
Hn.
Tpt.
Ten. Tbn. 1
Ten. Tbn. 2
Bass Tbn.
Timp.
Pros.
Rufe die Qualen aus stygischen Nächten empor!
Summon up the torments up from Stygian nights!
Vln. I
Vln. II
Vla.
Vc.
Db.

576
Fl.
Ob.
Cl.
Bsn.
Hn.
Tpt.
Ten. Tbn. 1
Ten. Tbn. 2
Bass Tbn.
Timp.
Sie steigen deinem Wink entgegen,
Nicht meine Liebe.
Pros.
They rise up at your bidding,
Not my love.
Vln. I
Vln. II
Vla.
Vc.
Db.

578
Fl.
Ob.
Cl.
Bsn.
Hn.
Tpt.
Ten. Tbn. 1
Ten. Tbn. 2
Bass Tbn.
Timp.
Pros.
Wie haß ich dich Abscheu und Gemahl,
How I hate you Horror and husband,
Vln. I
Vln. II
Vla.
Vc.
Db.
ff
pp

579
Fl.
Ob.
Cl.
Bsn.
Hn.
Tpt.
Ten. Tbn. 1
Ten. Tbn. 2
Bass Tbn.
Timp.
Pros.
O Pluto! Pluto!
Gib mir das Schicksal deiner Verdammten!
O Pluto! Pluto!
Give me the fate of your damned!
Vln. I
Vln. II
Vla.
Vc.
Db.

581
Fl.
Ob.
Cl.
Bsn.
Hn.
Tpt.
Ten. Tbn. 1
Ten. Tbn. 2
Bass Tbn.
(tr)
Timp.
Nenn es nicht Liebe!
Pros.
Do not call it love!
Vln. I
Vln. II
Vla.
Vc.
Db.

583
Fl.
Ob.
Cl.
Bsn.
Hn.
Tpt.
Ten. Tbn. 1
Ten. Tbn. 2
Bass Tbn.
Timp.
Pros.
Wirf mich mit diesen Armen in die zerstörende Qual!
Throw me with these arms into the destructive torment.
Vln. I
Vln. II
Vla.
Vc.
Db.

585
a2
Fl.
Ob.
Cl.
Bsn.
Hn.
Tpt.
Ten. Tbn. 1
Ten. Tbn. 2
Bass Tbn.
Timp.
Un - ser! Un - ser! Ho - he Kö - ni - gin!
You are ours now! No - ble hon - oured queen!
Vln. I
Vln. II
Vla.
Vc.
Db.
f
pp
fpp

588
Fl.
Ob.
Cl.
Bsn.
Hn.
Tpt.
Ten. Tbn. 1
Ten. Tbn. 2
Bass Tbn.
Timp.
Vln. I
Vln. II
Vla.
Vc.
Db.
a2
f cresc.
ff
p cresc.
tr
Db
Vcl.

Proserpina

Goethe's Melodrama
Music by Carl Eberwein

Piano Reduction & Translation

Proserpina

Johann Wolfgang von Goethe
(1749 - 1832)

Carl Eberwein
(1786 -1868)

sfp
Allegro assai
pp
p
Adagio

Tempo I°
f
lh

67
sf
sf
71
p
76
p
lh
p
80
84

89
95
f
100
105
110

137
fp
141
p
fp
p
146
151
156
f

Adagio
Tempo I°

185
190
195
200
sf
sf
204
sf
sf

210
p
p
Ped.
sim.
217
223
226
230

235
f
238
242
246
250

255

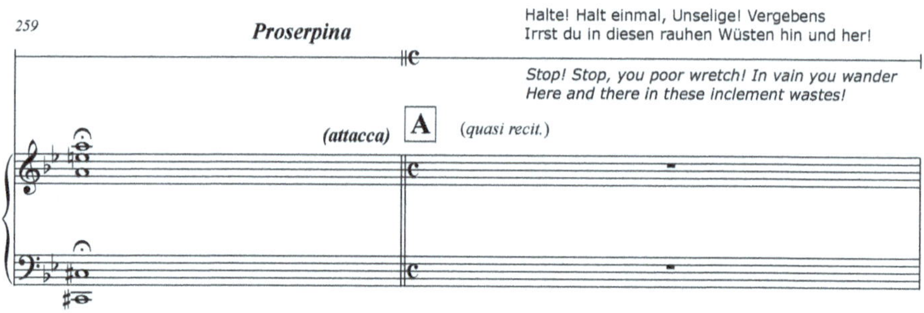
259
Proserpina
Halte! Halt einmal, Unselige! Vergebens
Irrst du in diesen rauhen Wüsten hin und her!
Stop! Stop, you poor wretch! In vain you wander
Here and there in these inclement wastes!
(attacca)
A
(quasi recit.)

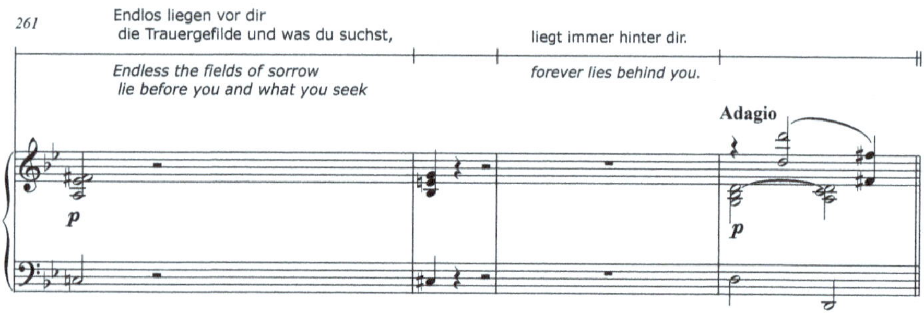
261
Endlos liegen vor dir
die Trauergefilde und was du suchst,
liegt immer hinter dir.
Endless the fields of sorrow
lie before you and what you seek
forever lies behind you.
Adagio
p
p

265

Nicht vorwärts,
Aufwärts auch soll dieser Blick nicht steigen!
Die schwarze Höhle des Tartarus
Verwölbt die lieben Gegenden des Himmels,
In die ich sonst
Nach meines Ahnherrn froher Wohnung
Mit Liebesblick hinaufsah!

Neither forward
Nor upward shall this glance rise!
The black cave of Tartarus enshrouds with
Cloudy cover the dear regions of heaven
To which I would
Look up to see with loving eyes
My ancestor's happy dwelling!

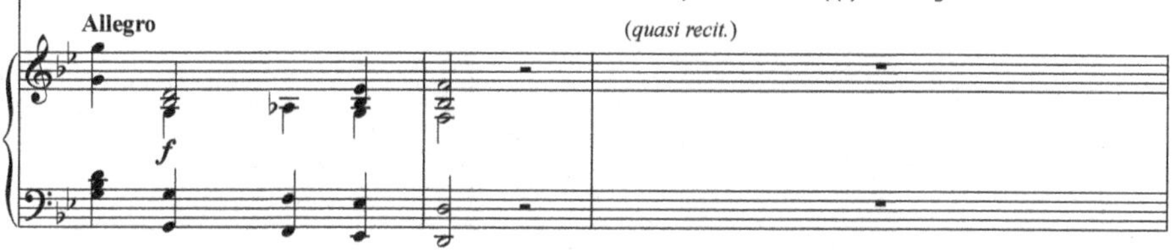

268

Ach! Tochter du des Jupiters,

Alas, daughter of Jupiter,

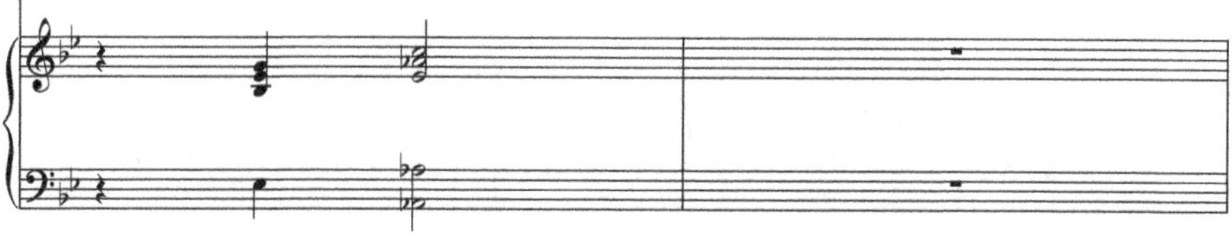

270

Wie tief bist du verloren!

How deeply you are lost!

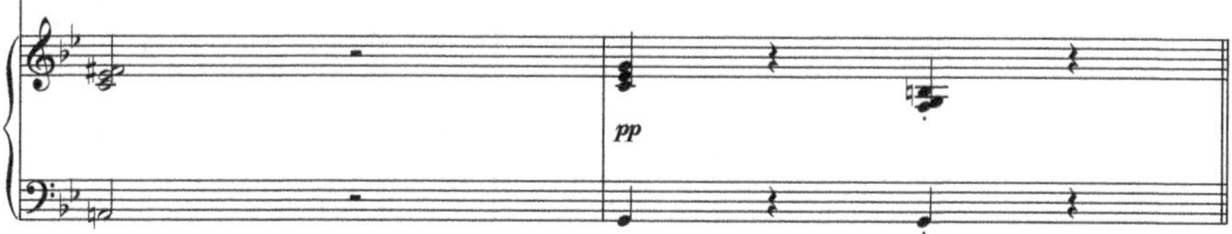

B

Andante

Gespielinnen!
Als jene blumenreiche Täler
Für uns gesamt noch blühten,
Als an dem himmelklaren Strom des Alpheus
Wir plätschernd noch im Abendstrahle scherzten,
Einander Kränze wanden
Und heimlich an den Jüngling dachten,
Dessen Haupt unser Herz sie widmete,
Da war uns keine Nacht zu tief zum Schwätzen,
Keine Zeit zu lang,
Um freundliche Geschichten zu wiederholen,
Und die Sonne
Riß leichter nicht aus ihrem Silberbette
Sich auf, als wir, voll Lust zu leben,
290 Früh im Tau die Rosenfüße badeten.

Playmates!
When those valleys, rich in flowers,
Still blossomed for us all,
When we splashed and laughed in the evening
Sun by the heavenly clear stream of Alpheus,
Wove garlands for each other,
And secretly recalled the youth
To whom our heart dedicated them:
Then no night was too deep for our conversation,
No hour too long
For the retelling of friendly stories,
And the sun
Did not rise more easily out of its silver bed
Than we returned early, full of joy for life,
To bathe our rosy feet in the dew.

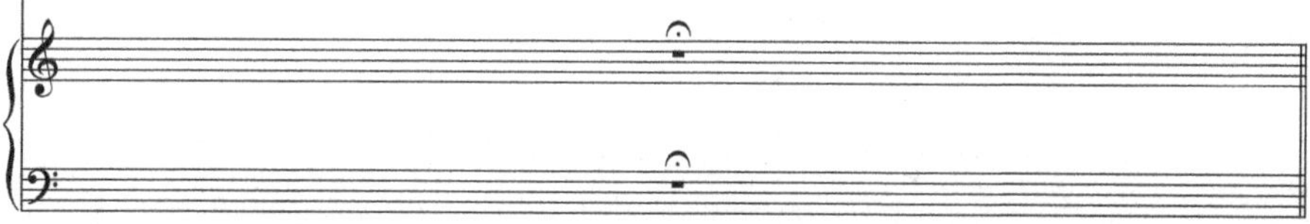

un poco piu Allegro

291

296

O Mädchen! Mädchen!
Die ihr, einsam nun,
Zerstreut an jenen Quellen schleicht,
Die Blumen auflest,
Die ich, ach, Entführte!
Aus meinem Schoße fallen ließ,
Ihr steht und seht mir nach,
wohin ich verschwand

O maidens, maidens!
Who wander alone,
Absent-minded by those streams,
Gathering the flowers
That I, alas, the abducted,
Let fall from my lap,
You stop to look for me,
To see whither I disappeared.

C **Allegro assai**

298

300

Weggerissen haben sie mich, die raschen Pferde des Orkus;

The swift horses of Arcus snatched me away;

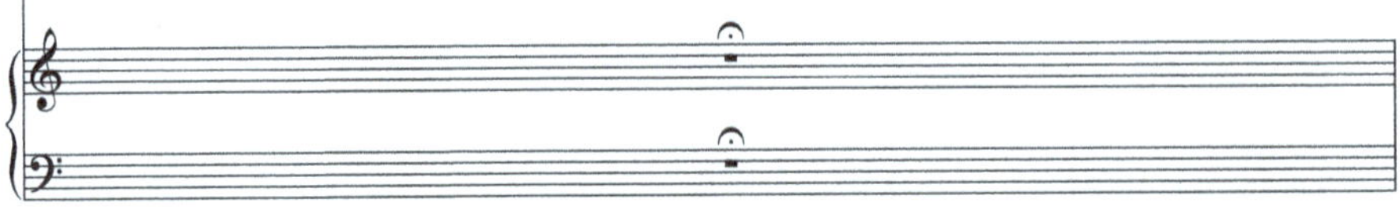

301

Mit festen Armen
Hielt mich der unerbittliche Gott!

With firm arms
The merciless God held me tight!

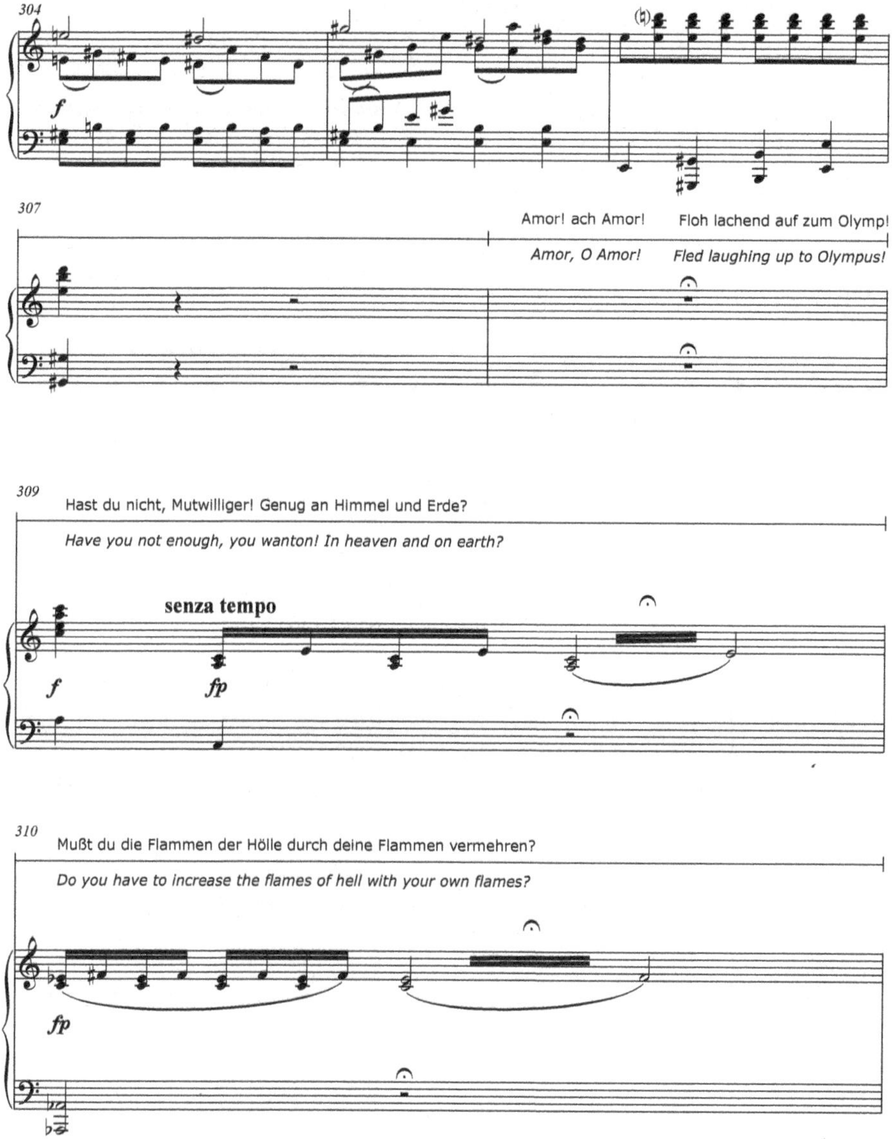
304
f
307
Amor! ach Amor!
Floh lachend auf zum Olymp!
Amor, O Amor!
Fled laughing up to Olympus!
309
Hast du nicht, Mutwilliger! Genug an Himmel und Erde?
Have you not enough, you wanton! In heaven and on earth?
senza tempo
f
fp
310
Mußt du die Flammen der Hölle durch deine Flammen vermehren?
Do you have to increase the flames of hell with your own flames?
fp

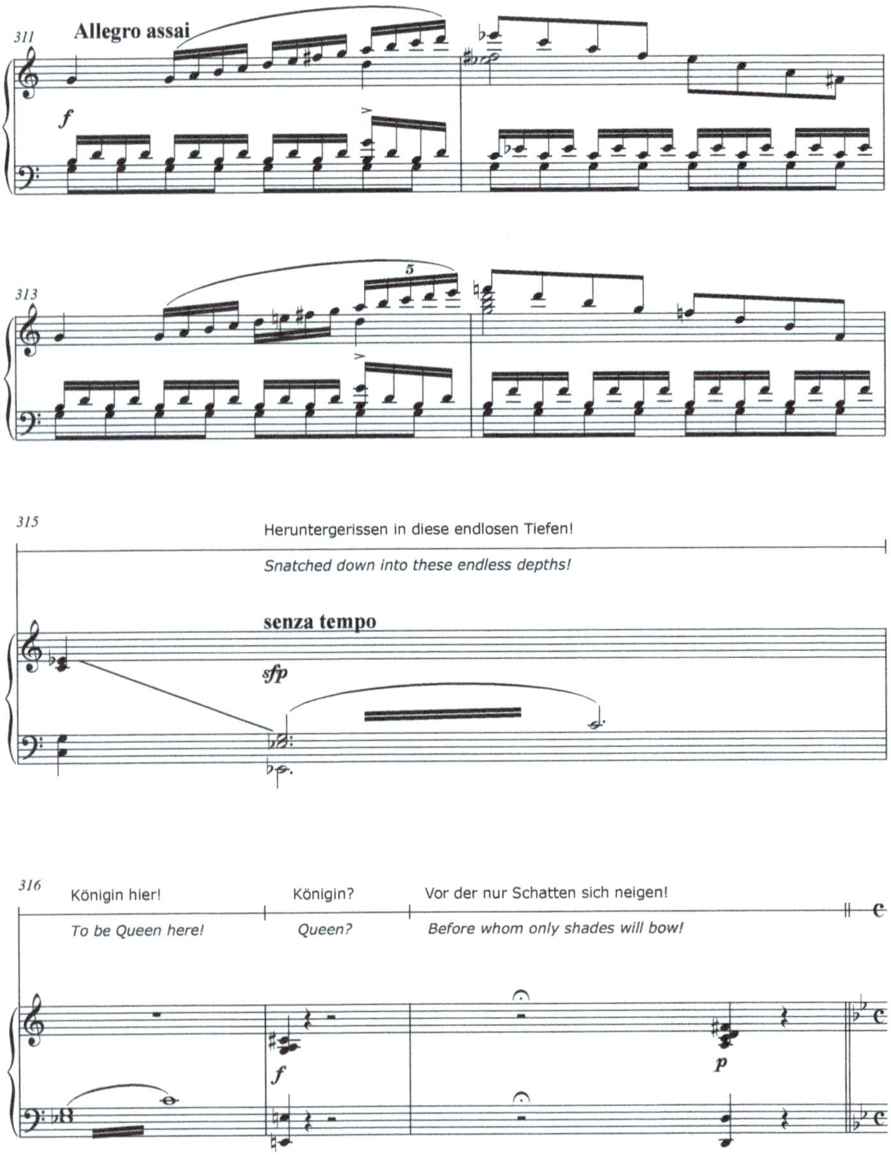
311
Allegro assai
f
313
5
315
Heruntergerissen in diese endlosen Tiefen!
Snatched down into these endless depths!
senza tempo
sfp
316
Königin hier!
To be Queen here!
Königin?
Queen?
Vor der nur Schatten sich neigen!
Before whom only shades will bow!
f
p

325

Hoffnungslos ist ihr Schmerz!
Hoffnungslos der Abgeschiedenen Glück,
Und ich wend es nicht.
Den ernsten Gerichten
Hat das Schicksal sie übergeben;
Und unter ihnen wandl' ich umher,
Göttin! Königin!
Selbst Sklavin des Schicksals!

Hopeless is their pain!
Hopeless the fate of the departed,
And I cannot change it;
Fate has handed them over
To the grim courts.
And among them I wander about,
Goddess, queen,
Myself a slave of fate!

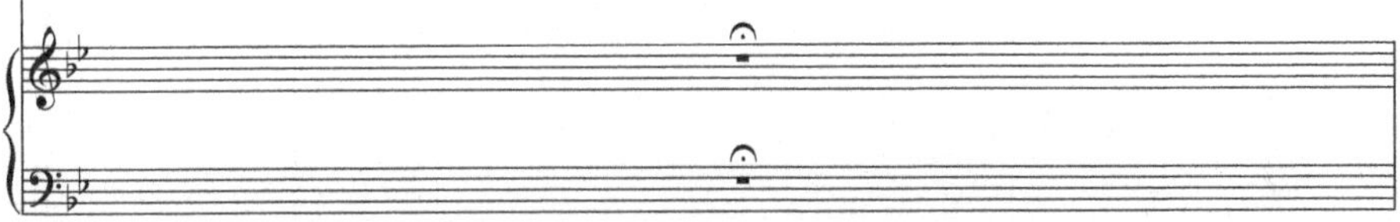

333 Ach, das fliehende Wasser
Möcht ich dem Tantalus schöpfen,

Oh, I would like to draw the fleeing water
For Tantalus!

Mit lieblichen Früchten ihn sättigen!
Armer Alter!
Für gereiztes Verlangen gestraft!

Satisfy him with sweet fruits!
Poor old man,
Punished for provoked craving!

337 In Ixions Rad möcht ich greifen,
Einhalten seinen Schmerz!

I would like to stop Ixion's wheel
And put an end to his pain!

Aber was vermögen wir Götter
Über die ewigen Qualen!

But what can we gods do
Against eternal punishment!

341 Trostlos für mich und für sie,
Wohn ich unter ihnen und schaue
Der armen Danaiden Geschäftigkeit!

I dwell here without hope for myself or them
And look at the work
Of the poor Danaids!

Leer und immer leer!
Wie sie schöpfen und füllen!

Empty and always empty,
How they draw and fill!

*This section down to figure [E] is basically Andante, apart from bars 337-38. The couplet 'In Ixions Rad möcht ich greifen, /Einhalten seinen Schmerz!' must coincide with these two Allegro bars. Otherwise a certain liberty can be taken with the placing of the text in order to allow the meaning and signicance of the words to come across in performance

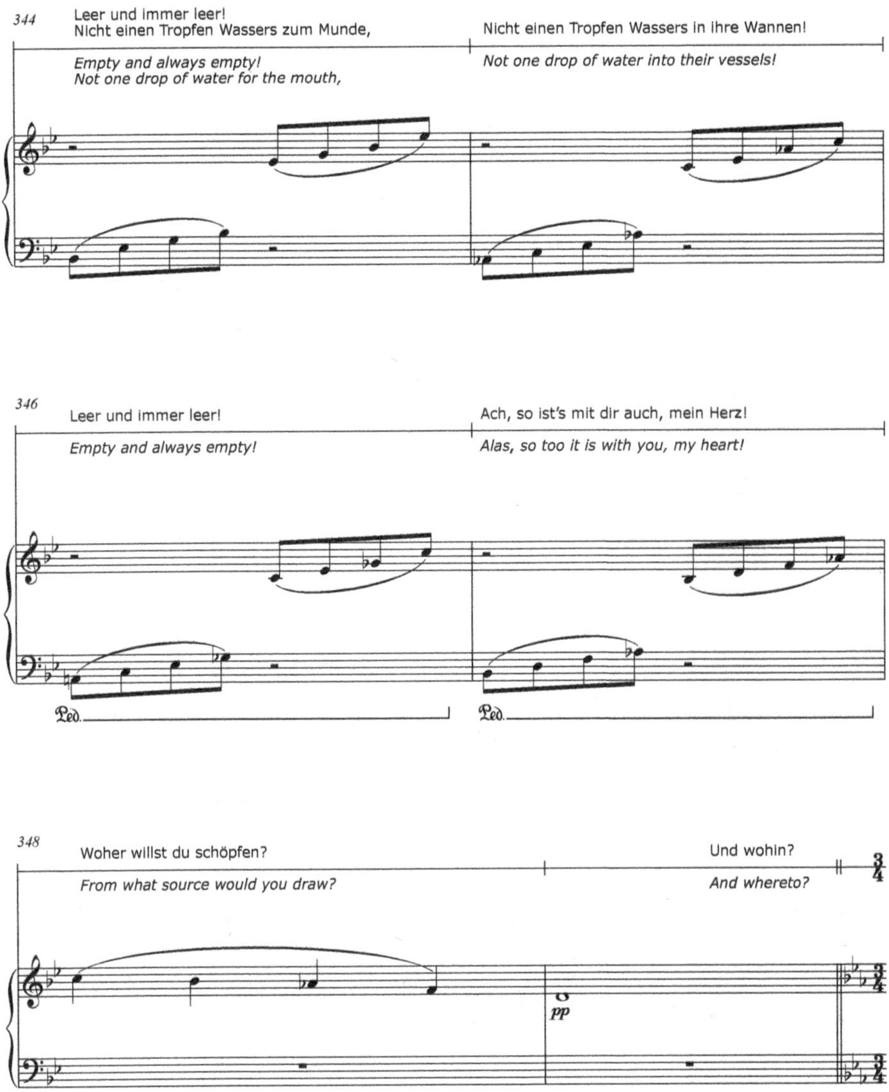
344
Leer und immer leer!
Nicht einen Tropfen Wassers zum Munde,
Empty and always empty!
Not one drop of water for the mouth,
Nicht einen Tropfen Wassers in ihre Wannen!
Not one drop of water into their vessels!
346
Leer und immer leer!
Empty and always empty!
Ach, so ist's mit dir auch, mein Herz!
Alas, so too it is with you, my heart!
Ped.
Ped.
348
Woher willst du schöpfen?
From what source would you draw?
Und wohin?
And whereto?
pp

358

Euer ruhiges Wandeln, Selige,
Streicht nur vor mir vorüber;
Mein Weg ist nicht mit euch!

Your quiet strolling, dead and departed,
Passes me by;
My way is not with you!

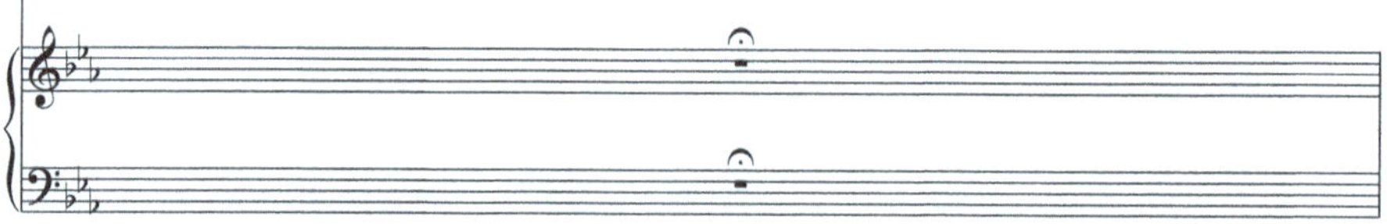

359

In euren leichten Tänzen,

In your playful dances,

In euren tiefen Hainen,

In your deep groves,

362
In eurer lispelnden Wohnung
In your whispering dwelling
5
365
Rauscht's nicht von Leben wie droben,
The teeming sounds of life are silent,
Schwankt nicht von Schmerz zu Lust
There is no vascillation from grief
367
Der Seligkeit Fülle.
To full bliss.

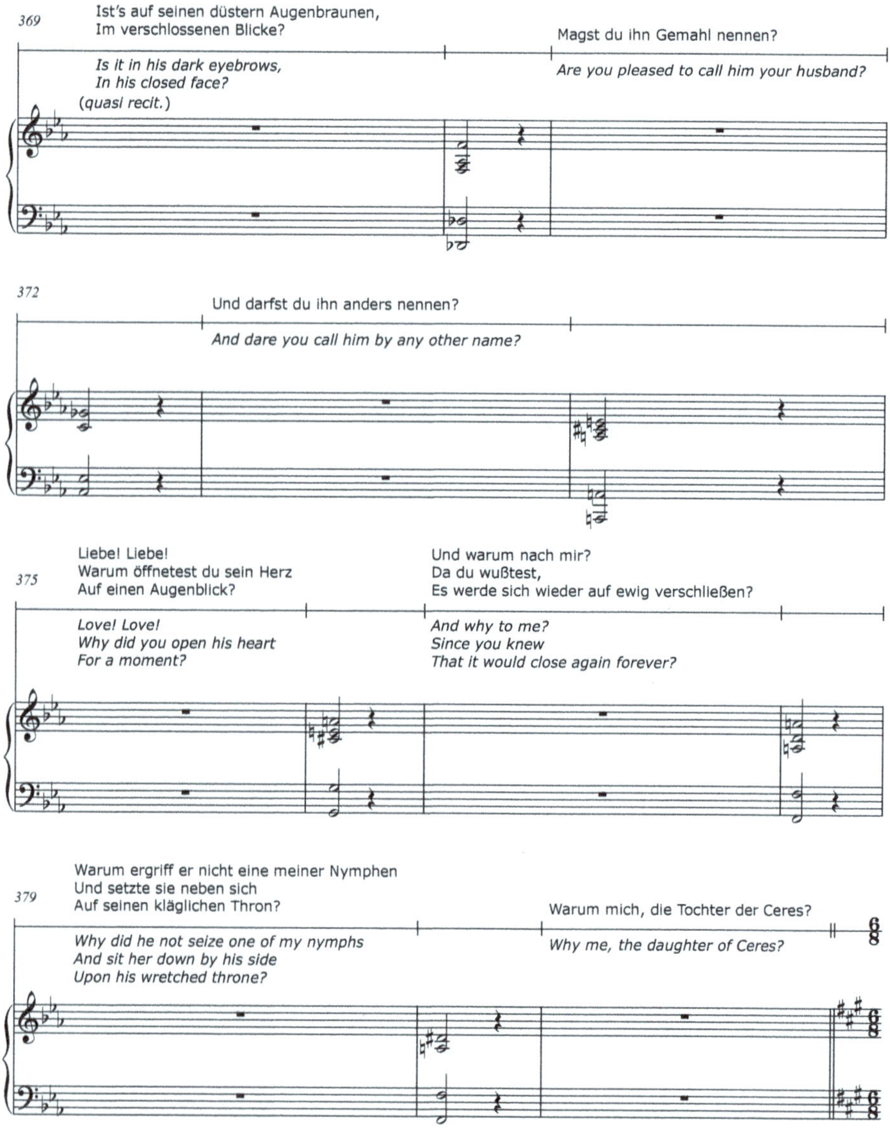
369
Ist's auf seinen düstern Augenbraunen,
Im verschlossenen Blicke?
Magst du ihn Gemahl nennen?
Is it in his dark eyebrows,
In his closed face?
Are you pleased to call him your husband?
(quasi recit.)
372
Und darfst du ihn anders nennen?
And dare you call him by any other name?
375
Liebe! Liebe!
Warum öffnetest du sein Herz
Auf einen Augenblick?
Und warum nach mir?
Da du wußtest,
Es werde sich wieder auf ewig verschließen?
Love! Love!
Why did you open his heart
For a moment?
And why to me?
Since you knew
That it would close again forever?
379
Warum ergriff er nicht eine meiner Nymphen
Und setzte sie neben sich
Auf seinen kläglichen Thron?
Warum mich, die Tochter der Ceres?
Why did he not seize one of my nymphs
And sit her down by his side
Upon his wretched throne?
Why me, the daughter of Ceres?

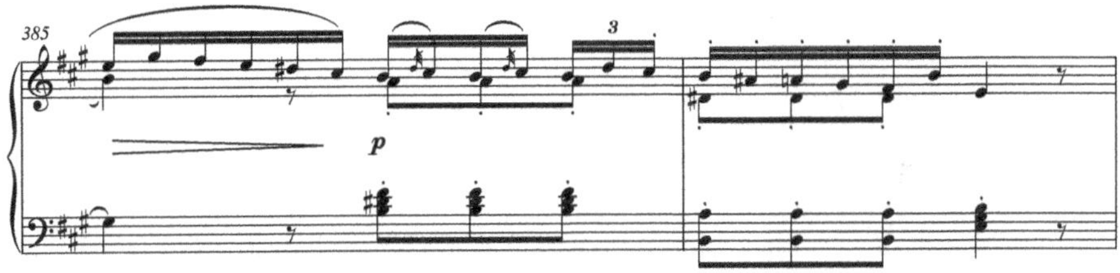

387

O Mutter! Mutter!
Wie dich deine Gottheit verläßt
Im Verlust deiner Tochter,
Die du glücklich glaubtest,
Hinspielend, hintändelnd ihre Jugend!

O mother! mother!
How your divinity forsakes you
At the loss of your daughter,
Whom you believed to be happy,
Playing, dallying away my youth!

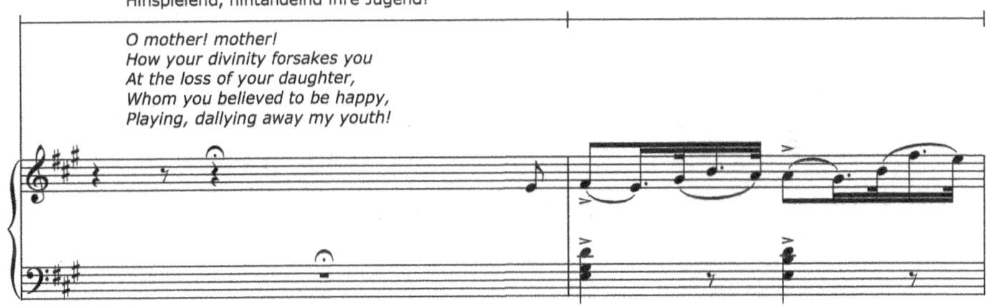

392

Ach, du kamst gewiß
Und fragtest nach mir,
Was ich bedürfte,
Etwa ein neues Kleid
Oder goldne Schuhe?

Oh, yes you came,
And asked about me
What I might need,
Perhaps a new gown
Or golden shoes?

394

Und du fandest die Mädchen
An ihre Weiden gefesselt,
Wo sie mich verloren,
Nicht wieder fanden,

And you found the maidens
Tied to their willows,
Where they lost me
And did not find me,

Ihre Locken zerrauften,

Tearing their hair out,

Erbärmlich klagten,

Lamenting pitifully,

396

meine lieben Mädchen!

My dear maidens!

398
G Allegro vivace
'Wohin ist sie? Wohin?', rufst du.
'Where has she gone? Where?', you cry.
(quasi recit.)
ff
400
'Welchen Weg nahm der Verruchte?
'What path did the scoundrel take?
Soll er ungestraft Jupiters Stamm entweihen?
Shall he, unpunished, desecrate Jupiter's line?
402
Wohin geht der Pfad seiner Rosse?
Where does the trail of his horses lead?
Fackeln her! Durch die Nacht will ich ihn verfolgen!
Torches here! In the night I will pursue him!
405
Will keine Stunde ruhen, bis ich sie finde,
I will not rest a single hour until I find her,
Will keinen Gang scheuen
I will eschew no path
Hierhin und dorthin!'
Here or there!'
f

H
Presto
408
p
p cresc.
mf
f
412
Dir blinken deine Drachen mit klugen Augen zu,
Aller Pfade gewohnt, folgen sie deinem Lenken:
In der unbewohnten
Wüste treibt dich's irre —
Your dragons look at you with knowing eyes;
Accustomed to all paths, they follow your lead:
You are driven astray
in uninhabited deserts —
(quasi recit.)
414
[Presto]
p
417
420
f

423

Ach, nur hierher, hierher nicht!
Nicht in die Tiefe der Nacht,
Unbetreten den Ewiglebenden,
Wo, bedeckt von beschwerendem Graus,
Deine Tochter ermattet!

Oh, only not here, not here
Not into the depths of the night.
Untrodden by the eternal gods, where,
Overburdened by the horror,
Your daughter languishes!

427

Wende aufwärts!
Aufwärts den geflügelten Schlangenpfad,

Turn upward!
Upward on the winged, winding path,

Aufwärts nach Jupiters Wohnung!

Upward to Jupiter's dwelling!

430

Der weiß es, der allein, der Erhabene,
Wo deine Tochter ist!

He knows it, the great god, he alone knows
Where your daughter is.

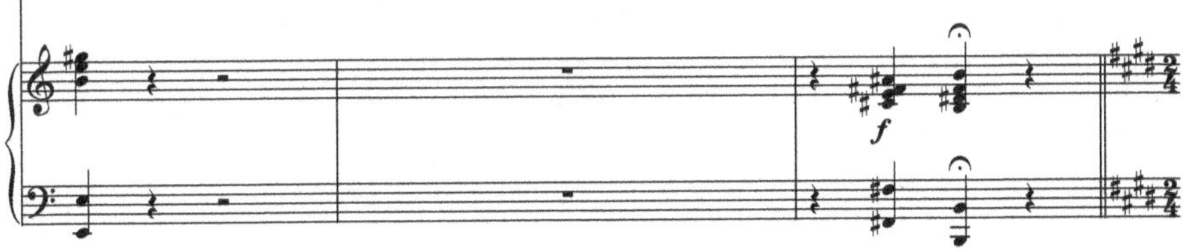

I **Larghetto**

433

Vater der Götter und Menschen!
Ruhst du noch oben auf deinem goldenen Stuhle,
Zu dem du mich Kleine
So oft mit Freundlichkeit aufhobst,
In deinen Händen mich scherzend
Gegen den endlosen Himmel schwenktest,
Daß ich kindisch droben zu verschweben bebte?
Bist du's noch, Vater? –

437

Father of gods and men!
Do you sit even now above on your golden throne
To which you so often raised me up
When I was little, laughing and lovingly
Swinging me in your arms
Toward the infinite sky, so that I, child that I was
Feared to stay hovering up there?
Are you still there, father?

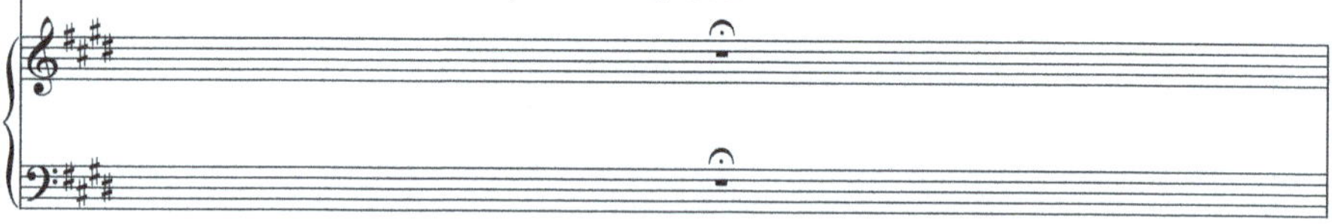

Nicht zu deinem Haupte
In dem ewigen Blau
Des feuerdurchwebten Himmels,
Hier! Hier! —

438

Not to you
In the eternal blue skies
Lit up with fire,
But here, here! —

Leite sie her!
Daß ich auf mit ihr
Aus diesem Kerker fahre!
Daß mir Phöbus wieder
Seine lieben Strahlen bringe,
Luna wieder
Aus den Silberlocken lächle!

444

Guide her here,
That I may ride up with her
Out of this dungeon!
That Phoebus may bring me
His lovely rays once more,
That Luna may smile at me again
From her silvery tresses!

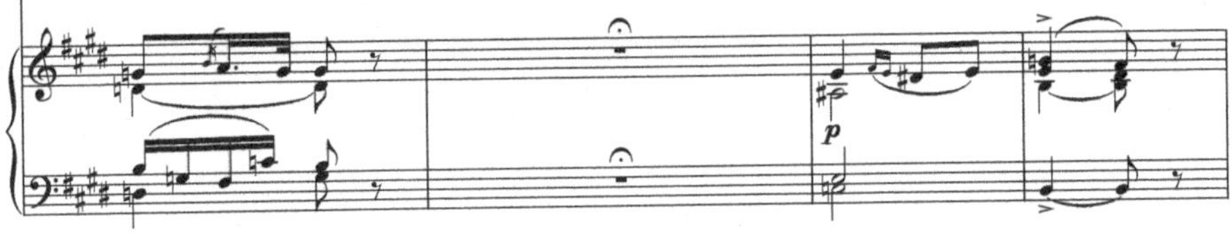

O du hörst mich,
Freundlichlieber Vater,
Wirst mich wieder,
Wieder aufwärts heben;
Daß, befreit von langer, schwerer Plage,
Ich an deinem Himmel wieder mich ergetze!

448

O, you hear me,
Dear father and friend,
And will raise me up
Again, again:
So that freed from long and dire torment,
I may take delight in your heaven!

450

Letze dich, verzagtes Herz!
Ach! Hoffnung!
Hoffnung gießt
In Sturmnacht Morgenröte!

Be refreshed, despondent heart!
Oh! Hope!
Hope pours the sunrise
Into the stormy night!

456

Dieser Boden ist nicht Fels,
Nicht Moos mehr;

This ground is not rock,
No longer moss,

Diese Berge
Nicht voll schwarzen Grauses!

These mountains
Are not full of black horror!

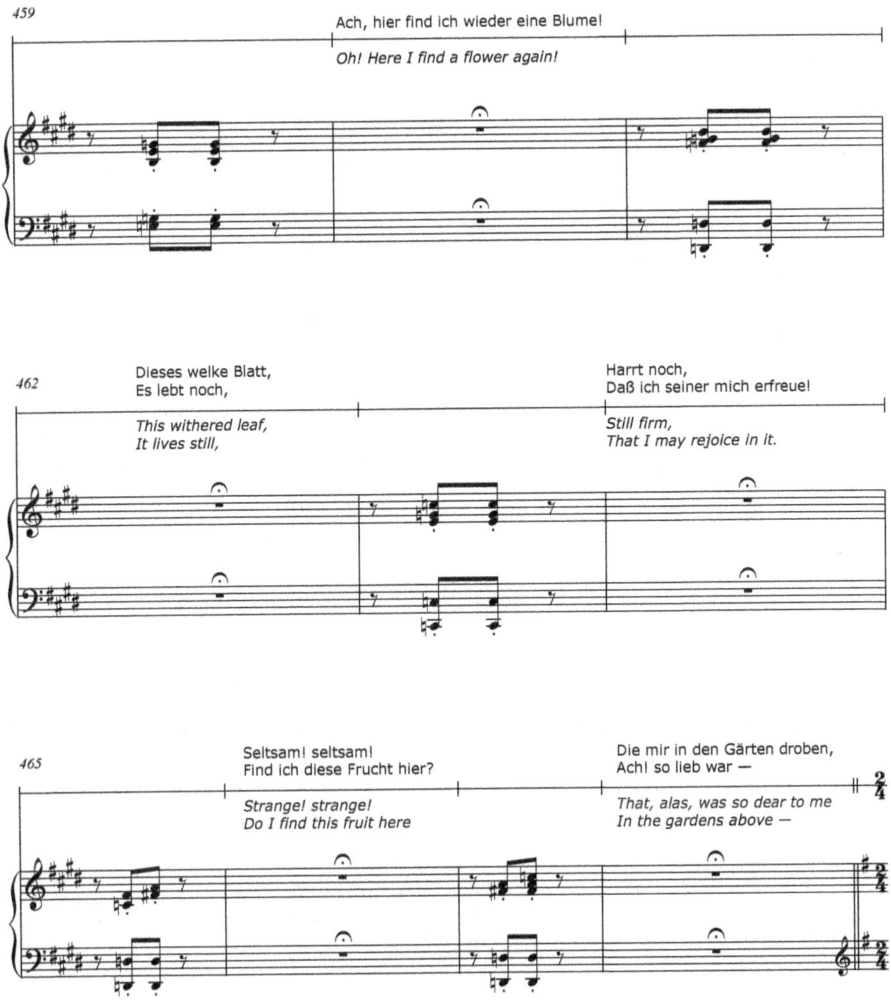
459
Ach, hier find ich wieder eine Blume!
Oh! Here I find a flower again!
462
Dieses welke Blatt,
Es lebt noch,
This withered leaf,
It lives still,
Harrt noch,
Daß ich seiner mich erfreue!
Still firm,
That I may rejoice in it.
465
Seltsam! seltsam!
Find ich diese Frucht hier?
Strange! strange!
Do I find this fruit here
Die mir in den Gärten droben,
Ach! so lieb war —
That, alas, was so dear to me
In the gardens above —

J **Andantino quasi Allegretto**

(Sie bricht den Granatapfel ab.)
(She breaks open the pomegranate)

Laß dich genießen,
Freundliche Frucht!
Laß mich vergessen
Alle den Harm!
Wieder mich wähnen
Droben in Jugend,
In der vertaumelten
Lieblichen Zeit,
In den umduftenden
Himmlischen Blüten,
In den Gerüchen
Seliger Wonne,
Die der Entzückten,
Der Schmachtenden ward!

478

Let me savour you,
Friendly fruit!
Let me forget
All my sorrow!
Let me pretend
I am above
In my youth again
The whirl of
Those lovely days,
Amid the fragrant
Heavenly flowers,
Amid the fragrances
Of joyful bliss
That I, ravished and languished,
Once knew!

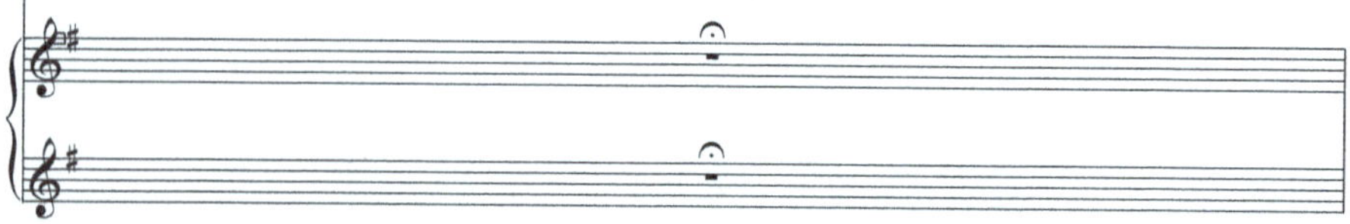

479
(Sie ißt einige Körner)
(She eats some seeds)
p

483
Labend!
Refreshing!
Labend!
Refreshing!
6

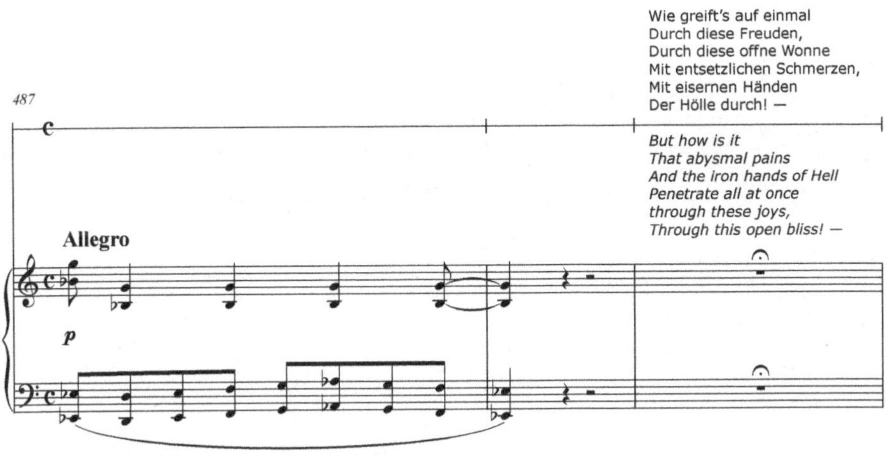
487
Allegro
p
Wie greift's auf einmal
Durch diese Freuden,
Durch diese offne Wonne
Mit entsetzlichen Schmerzen,
Mit eisernen Händen
Der Hölle durch! —
But how is it
That abysmal pains
And the iron hands of Hell
Penetrate all at once
through these joys,
Through this open bliss! —

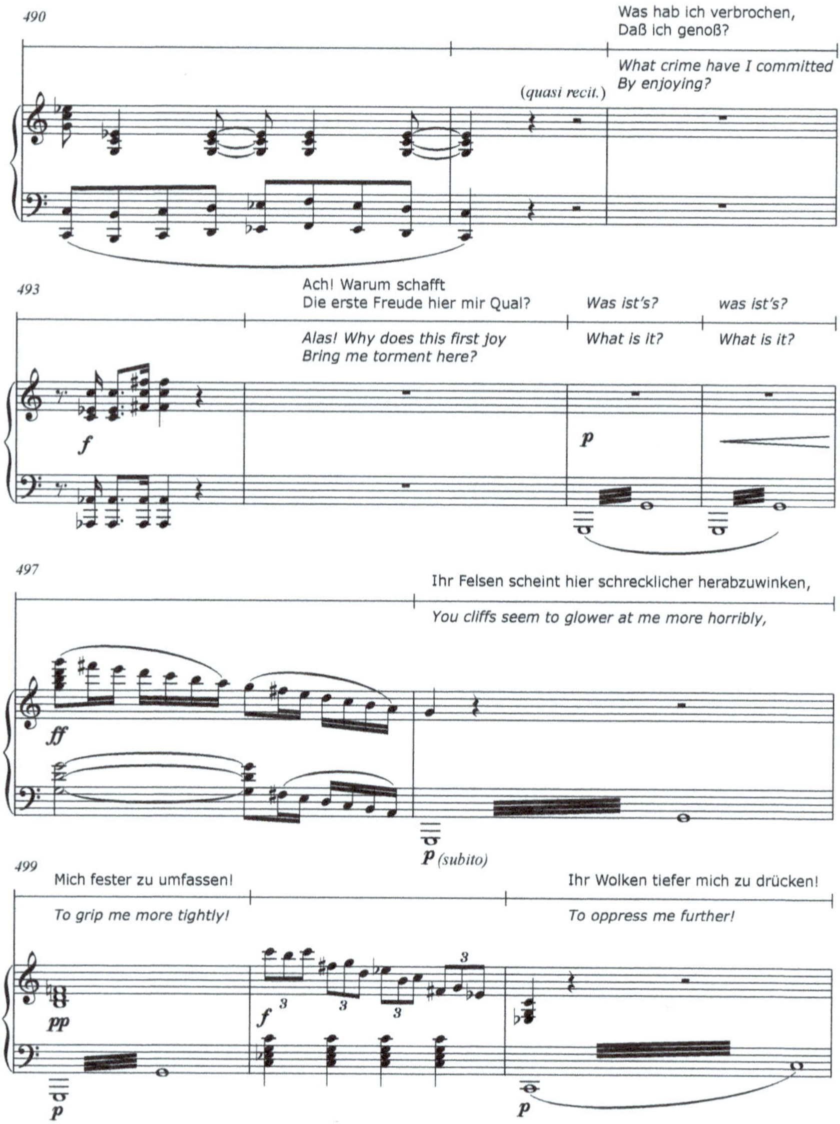
490
Was hab ich verbrochen,
Daß ich genoß?
What crime have I committed
By enjoying?
(quasi recit.)
493
Ach! Warum schafft
Die erste Freude hier mir Qual?
Alas! Why does this first joy
Bring me torment here?
Was ist's?
What is it?
was ist's?
What is it?
497
Ihr Felsen scheint hier schrecklicher herabzuwinken,
You cliffs seem to glower at me more horribly,
(subito)
499
Mich fester zu umfassen!
To grip me more tightly!
Ihr Wolken tiefer mich zu drücken!
To oppress me further!

502 Im fernen Schoße des Abgrunds
Dumpfe Gewitter tosend sich zu erzeugen!

In the depths of the abyss,
Muted thunderstorms begin to roll!

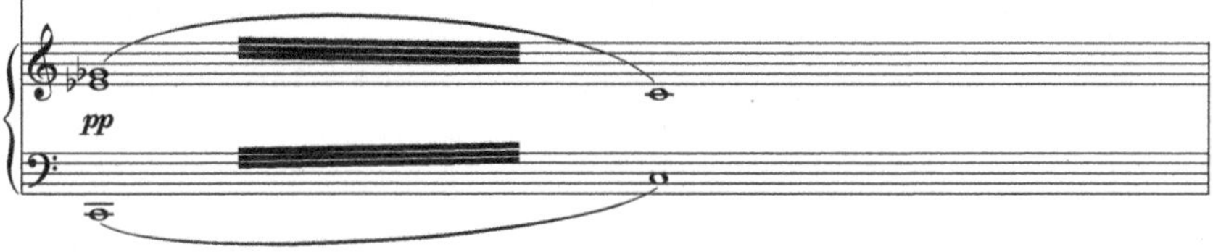

503 Und ihr weiten Reiche der Parzen

And you vast regions of the Fates

[Allegro]

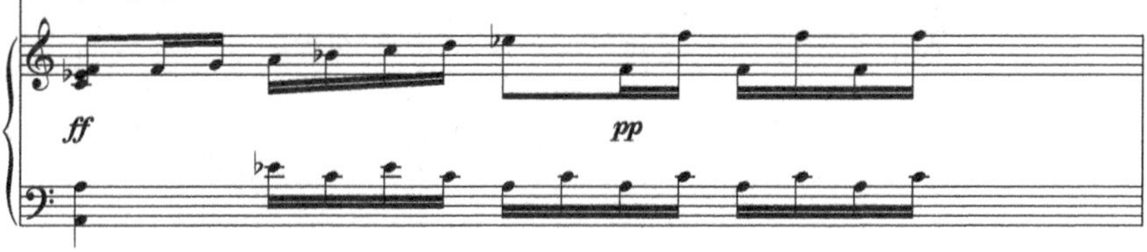

504 Mir zuzurufen: Du bist unser!

Seem to call to me: You are ours!

506

K Adagio
Chorus DIE PARZEN (unsichtbar)
The Fates (off-stage)
CHOIR I
508
S A
T
B B
Du bist un - ser! Ist der Rat - schluß dei - nes Ahn - herrn:
You are ours now! Your an - ces - tor has or - dained it so:
(for rehearsal only)
512
Nüch - tern soll - test wie - der - keh - ren; Und der Biß des Ap - fels macht dich
You were to re - turn here so - ber; And the bite of ap - ple makes you

515
un - ser! Kö - ni-gin, Kö - ni - gin, wir ehr - en dich!
ours now! Queen, we pay ho -mage now, we hon - our you!
un - ser! Kö - ni-gin, Kö - ni - gin, wir ehr - en dich!
ours now! Queen, we pay ho -mage now, we hon - our you!
un - ser! Kö - ni-gin, Kö - ni - gin, wir ehr - en dich!
ours now! Queen, we pay ho -mage now, we hon - our you!

520
Hast du's gesprochen, Vater
You have spoken, Father
Warum? warum?
Was tat ich, daß du mich verstößest?
Why? Why?
What did I do for you to cast me out?
L
Allegro
(quasi recit.)

523
Warum rufst du mich nicht
Zu deinem lichten Thron auf?
Why do you not call me up
To your radiant throne?
Warum den Apfel?
O verflucht die Früchte!
Why the pomegranate?
O curse the fruits!
f
525
Warum sind Früchte schön, wenn sie verdammen?
Why are fruits so beautiful if they bring damnation?
[Allegro]
f
M
Adagio
528
CHOIR II
S
A
T I
T II
B
f
Bist nun un - ser! Wa-rum trau-erst du? Sieh, wir ehr-en dich! Un - sre Kö-ni - gin!
You are ours now! Why do you la-ment? See, we hon-our you! You, our no-ble queen!
(for rehearsal only)

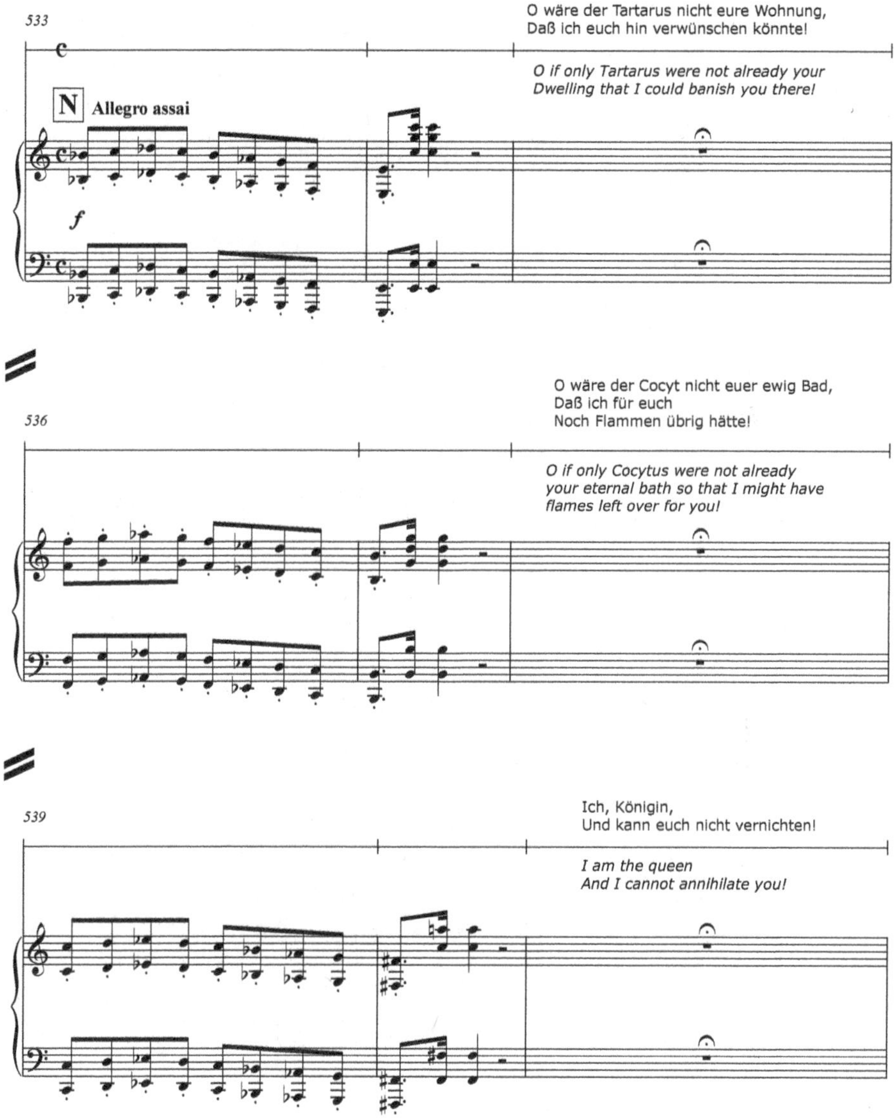
533
O wäre der Tartarus nicht eure Wohnung,
Daß ich euch hin verwünschen könnte!
O if only Tartarus were not already your
Dwelling that I could banish you there!
N
Allegro assai
f
536
O wäre der Cocyt nicht euer ewig Bad,
Daß ich für euch
Noch Flammen übrig hätte!
O if only Cocytus were not already
your eternal bath so that I might have
flames left over for you!
539
Ich, Königin,
Und kann euch nicht vernichten!
I am the queen
And I cannot annihilate you!

542

In ewigem Haß sei ich mit euch verbunden! -

May I be bound to you in eternal hatred! -

544

So schöpfet, Danaiden! Spinnt, Parzen!

So draw water, Danaids! Spin, Fates!

Wütet, Furien!
In ewig gleich elendem Schicksal!
Ich beherrsche euch
Und bin darum elender als ihr alle

Rage, Furies!
In an eternally wretched fate!
I govern you
And so am more wretched than you all.

O Adagio
550
S A
Du bist un - ser!
You are ours now!
Wir nei-gen uns dir!
We bow to — you!
T
Du bist un - ser!
You are ours now!
Wir nei-gen uns dir!
We bow to — you!
Bist
You are
unis.
B B
Du bist un - ser!
You are ours now!
Wir nei-gen uns dir!
We bow to — you!
Bist
You are
S A
Du bist un - ser!
You are ours now!
Wir nei-gen uns dir!
We bow to — you!
unis.
T T
Du bist un - ser!
You are ours now!
Wir nei-gen uns dir!
We bow to — you!
Bist
You are
B
Du bist un - ser!
You are ours now!
Wir nei-gen uns dir!
We bow to — you!
Bist
You are

555
Un - ser! Ho - he Kö - ni - gin!
Ours now! You, our no - ble queen!
un - ser! Un - ser! Ho - he Kö - ni - gin!
ours now! Ours now! You, our no - ble queen!
un - ser! Un - ser! Ho - he Kö - ni - gin!
ours now! Ours now! You, our no - ble queen!
Un - ser! Ho - he Kö - ni - gin!
Ours now! You, our no - ble queen!
un - ser! Un - ser! Ho - he Kö - ni - gin!
ours now! Ours now! You, our no - ble queen!
un - ser! Un - ser! Ho - he Kö - ni - gin!
ours now! Ours now! You, our no - ble queen!

559

Fern! weg von mir
Sei eure Treu und Herrlichkeit!

Away, away from me
with your fidelity and your glory!

562

Wie haß ich euch!
Und dich, wie zehnfach haß ich dich —

How I hate you!
And you, how I hate you tenfold —

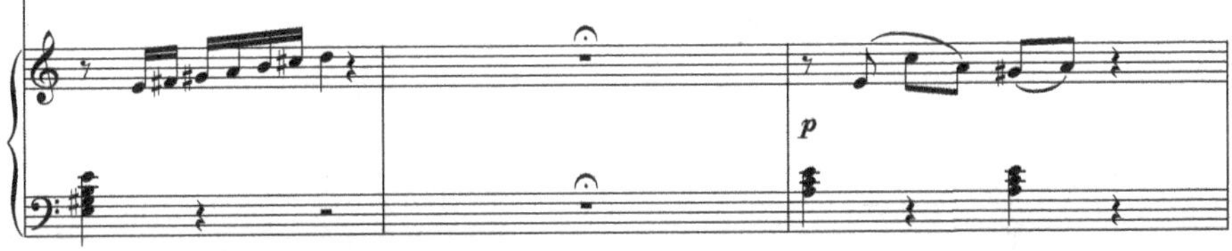

565 Weh mir! Ich fühle schon die verhaßten Umarmungen!

Woe is me! I already feel the abhorrent embraces.

CHOIRS I & II
567
SA
Un - ser! Un - sre Kö - ni - gin!
Ours now! You our no - ble queen!
TT
Un - ser! Un - sre Kö - ni - gin!
Ours now! You our no - ble queen!
BB
Un - ser! Un - sre Kö - ni - gin!
Ours now! You our no - ble queen!
571
Warum reckst du sie nach mir?
Recke sie nach dem Avernus!
Why do you stretch out your arms to me?
Stretch them out to Avernus!
574
Rufe die Qualen aus stygischen Nächten empor!
Summon up the torments up from Stygian nights!

576

Sie steigen deinem Wink entgegen,
Nicht meine Liebe.

They rise up at your bidding,
Not my love.

578

Wie haß ich dich
Abscheu und Gemahl,

O Pluto! Pluto! Gib mir das Schicksal deiner

How I hate you
Horror and husband,

O Pluto! Pluto! Give me the fate of your

580

Verdammten!

Nenn es nicht Liebe!

damned!

Do not call it love!

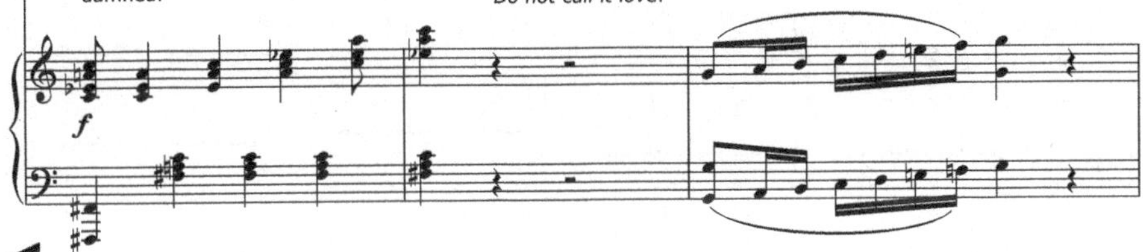

583

Wirf mich mit diesen Armen
In die zerstörende Qual!

Throw me with these arms
Into the destructive torment!

CHOIRS I & II
585
SA
f
Un - ser! Un - ser! Ho - he Kö - ni - gin!
You are ours now! No - ble hon - oured queen!
TT
f
Un - ser! Un - ser! Ho - he Kö - ni - gin!
You are ours now! No - ble hon - oured queen!
BB
f
Un - ser! Un - ser! Ho - he Kö - ni - gin!
You are ours now! No - ble hon - oured queen!
f pp
588
p
cresc.
590
ff
ff

Appendix 1

Proserpina. Ein Monodram

Johann Wolfgang von Goethe

Eine öde, felsigte Gegend,
Höhle im Grund, auf der einen Seite
ein Granatbaum mit Früchten.

PROSERPINA
Halte! Halt einmal, Unselige! Vergebens
Irrst du in diesen rauhen Wüsten hin und her!
Endlos liegen vor dir die Trauergefilde,
Und was du suchst, liegt immer hinter dir.

Nicht vorwärts,
Aufwärts auch soll dieser Blick nicht steigen!
Die schwarze Höhle des Tartarus
Verwölbt die lieben Gegenden des Himmels,
In die ich sonst
Nach meines Ahnherrn froher Wohnung
Mit Liebesblick hinaufsah!
Ach! Tochter du des Jupiters,
Wie tief bist du verloren!

Gespielinnen!
Als jene blumenreiche Täler
Für uns gesamt noch blühten,
Als an dem himmelklaren Strom des Alpheus
Wir plätschernd noch im Abendstrahle scherzten,
Einander Kränze wanden
Und heimlich an den Jüngling dachten,

Proserpina: A Monodrama

Johann Wolfgang von Goethe

A desolate, rocky region,
a cave in the background, on one side
a pomegranate tree with fruit.

PROSERPINA:
Stop! Stop, you poor wretch! In vain you wander
Here and there in these inclement wastes!
Endless the fields of sorrow lie before you
And what you seek forever lies behind you.

Neither forward
Nor upward shall this glance rise!
The black cave of Tartarus enshrouds with
Cloudy cover the dear regions of heaven
To which I would
Look up to see with loving eyes
My ancestor's happy dwelling!
Alas, daughter of Jupiter,
How deeply you are lost!

Playmates!
When those valleys, rich in flowers,
Still blossomed for us all,
When we splashed and laughed in the evening
Sun by the heavenly clear stream of Alpheus,
Wove garlands for each other,
And secretly recalled the youth

Dessen Haupt unser Herz sie widmete,
Da war uns keine Nacht zu tief zum Schwätzen,
Keine Zeit zu lang,
Um freundliche Geschichten zu wiederholen,
Und die Sonne
Riß leichter nicht aus ihrem Silberbette
Sich auf, als wir, voll Lust zu leben,
Früh im Tau die Rosenfüße badeten.

O Mädchen! Mädchen!
Die ihr, einsam nun,
Zerstreut an jenen Quellen schleicht,
Die Blumen auflest,
Die ich, ach, Entführte!
Aus meinem Schoße fallen ließ,
Ihr steht und seht mir nach,
wohin ich verschwand.

Weggerissen haben sie mich,
Die raschen Pferde des Orkus;
Mit festen Armen
Hielt mich der unerbittliche Gott!
Amor! ach Amor! floh lachend auf zum Olymp!
Hast du nicht, Mutwilliger!
Genug an Himmel und Erde?
Mußt du die Flammen der Hölle
Durch deine Flammen vermehren?

Heruntergerissen
In diese endlosen Tiefen!
Königin hier!
Königin?
Vor der nur Schatten sich neigen!

Hoffnungslos ist ihr Schmerz!
Hoffnungslos der Abgeschiedenen Glück,
Und ich wend es nicht.
Den ernsten Gerichten
Hat das Schicksal sie übergeben;
Und unter ihnen wandl' ich umher,
Göttin! Königin!
Selbst Sklavin des Schicksals!

Ach, das fliehende Wasser
Möcht ich dem Tantalus schöpfen,
Mit lieblichen Früchten ihn sättigen!
Armer Alter!
Für gereiztes Verlangen gestraft! –
In Ixions Rad möcht ich greifen,

To whom our heart dedicated them:
Then no night was too deep for our
conversation, no hour too long
For the retelling of friendly stories,
And the sun
Did not rise more easily out of its silver bed
Than we returned early, full of joy for life,
To bathe our rosy feet in the dew.

O maidens, maidens!
Who wander alone,
Absent-minded,
By those streams, gathering the flowers
That I, alas, the abducted,
Let fall from my lap,
You stop to look for me,
To see whither I disappeared.

The swift horses of Arcus;
Snatched me away
With firm arms
The merciless God held me tight!
Amor, O Amor! fled laughing up to Olympus!
Have you not enough, you wanton,
In heaven and on earth?
Do you have to increase the flames of hell
With your own flames?

Snatched down
Into these endless depths!
To be Queen here!
Queen?
Before whom only shades will bow!

Hopeless is their pain!
Hopeless the fate of the departed,
And I cannot change it;
Fate has handed them over
To the grim courts.
And among them I wander about,
Goddess, queen,
Myself a slave of fate!

Oh, I would like to draw the fleeing water
For Tantalus!
Satisfy him with sweet fruits!
Poor old man,
Punished for provoked craving!
I would like to stop Ixion's wheel

Einhalten seinen Schmerz!
Aber was vermögen wir Götter
Über die ewigen Qualen!
Trostlos für mich und für sie,
Wohn ich unter ihnen und schaue
Der armen Danaiden Geschäftigkeit!
Leer und immer leer!
Wie sie schöpfen und füllen!
Leer und immer leer!
Nicht einen Tropfen Wassers zum Munde,
Nicht einen Tropfen Wassers in ihre Wannen!
Leer und immer leer!
Ach, so ist's mit dir auch, mein Herz!
Woher willst du schöpfen?
Und wohin?
Euer ruhiges Wandeln, Selige,
Streicht nur vor mir vorüber;
Mein Weg ist nicht mit euch!
In euren leichten Tänzen,
In euren tiefen Hainen,
In eurer lispelnden Wohnung
Rauscht's nicht von Leben wie droben,
Schwankt nicht von Schmerz zu Lust
Der Seligkeit Fülle. –

Ist's auf seinen düstern Augenbraunen,
Im verschlossenen Blicke?
Magst du ihn Gemahl nennen?
Und darfst du ihn anders nennen?
Liebe! Liebe!
Warum öffnetest du sein Herz
Auf einen Augenblick?
Und warum nach mir?
Da du wußtest,
Es werde sich wieder auf ewig verschließen?
Warum ergriff er nicht eine meiner Nymphen
Und setzte sie neben sich
Auf seinen kläglichen Thron?
Warum mich, die Tochter der Ceres?

O Mutter! Mutter!
Wie dich deine Gottheit verläßt
Im Verlust deiner Tochter,
Die du glücklich glaubtest,
Hinspielend, hintändelnd ihre Jugend!

Ach, du kamst gewiß
Und fragtest nach mir,
Was ich bedürfte,

And put an end to his pain.
But what can we gods do
Against eternal punishment!
I dwell here without hope for myself or them
And look at the work
Of the poor Danaids.
Empty and always empty,
How they draw and fill!
Empty and always empty!
Not one drop of water for the mouth,
Not one drop of water into their vessels!
Empty and always empty!
Alas, so too it is with you, my heart!
From what source would you draw
And whereto?
Your quiet strolling, dead and departed,
Passes me by;
My way is not with you.
In your playful dances,
In your deep groves
In your whispering houses, the teeming sounds of life are silent;
There is no vascillation from grief
To full bliss.

Is it in his dark eyebrows,
In his closed face?
Are you pleased to call him your husband?
And dare you call him by any other name?
Love! Love!
Why did you open his heart
For a moment?
And why to me?
Since you knew
That it would close again forever?
Why did he not seize one of my nymphs
And sit her down by his side
Upon his wretched throne?
Why me, the daughter of Ceres?

O mother! mother!
How your divinity forsakes you
At the loss of your daughter,
Whom you believed to be happy,
Playing, dallying away my youth.

Oh, yes you came,
And asked after me
What I might need,

Etwa ein neues Kleid
Oder goldne Schuhe?
Und du fandest die Mädchen
An ihre Weiden gefesselt,
Wo sie mich verloren,
Nicht wieder fanden,
Ihre Locken zerrauften,
Erbärmlich klagten,
meine lieben Mädchen! –

'Wohin ist sie? Wohin?', rufst du
'Welchen Weg nahm der Verruchte?
Soll er ungestraft Jupiters Stamm entweihen?

Wohin geht der Pfad seiner Rosse?
Fackeln her!
Durch die Nacht will ich ihn verfolgen!
Will keine Stunde ruhen, bis ich sie finde,
Will keinen Gang scheuen
Hierhin und dorthin!'

Dir blinken deine Drachen mit klugen Augen zu,
Aller Pfade gewohnt, folgen sie deinem Lenken:
In der unbewohnten Wüste treibt dich's irre –

Ach, nur hierher, hierher nicht!
Nicht in die Tiefe der Nacht,
Unbetreten den Ewiglebenden,
Wo, bedeckt von beschwerendem Graus,
Deine Tochter ermattet!

Wende aufwärts!
Aufwärts den geflügelten Schlangenpfad,
Aufwärts nach Jupiters Wohnung!
Der weiß es,
Der weiß es, der allein, der Erhabene,
Wo deine Tochter ist! –

Vater der Götter und Menschen!
Ruhst du noch oben auf deinem goldenen Stuhle,
Zu dem du mich Kleine
So oft mit Freundlichkeit aufhobst,
In deinen Händen mich scherzend
Gegen den endlosen Himmel schwenktest,
Daß ich kindisch droben zu verschweben bebte?
Bist du's noch, Vater? –

Nicht zu deinem Haupte
In dem ewigen Blau

Perhaps a new gown
Or golden shoes?
And you found the maidens
Tied to their willows,
Where they lost me
And did not find me,
Tearing their hair out,
Lamenting pitifully,
My dear maidens!

'Where has she gone? Where?', you cry.
'What path did the scoundrel take?
Shall he, unpunished, desecrate Jupiter's line?

Where does the trail of his horses lead?
Torches here!
In the night I will pursue him!
I will not rest a single hour until I find her,
I will eschew no path
Here or there!'

Your dragons look at you with knowing eyes;
Accustomed to all paths, they follow your lead:
You are driven astray in uninhabited deserts –

Oh, only not here, not here!
Not into the depths of the night.
Untrodden by the eternal gods, where
Overburdened by the horror,
Your daughter languishes!

Turn upward!
Upward on the winged, winding path,
Upward to Jupiter's dwelling!
He knows it,
The great god, he alone knows
Where your daughter is.

Father of gods and men!
Do you sit even now above on your golden
Throne, to which you so often raised me up
When I was little, laughingly and lovingly
Swinging me in your arms
Toward the infinite sky, so that I, child that I
Was, feared to stay hovering up there?
Are you still there, father?

Not to you
In the eternal blue skies

Des feuerdurchwebten Himmels,
Hier! Hier! –

Leite sie her!
Daß ich auf mit ihr
Aus diesem Kerker fahre!

Daß mir Phöbus wieder
Seine lieben Strahlen bringe,
Luna wieder
Aus den Silberlocken lächle!

O du hörst mich,
Freundlichlieber Vater,
Wirst mich wieder,
Wieder aufwärts heben;
Daß, befreit von langer, schwerer Plage,
Ich an deinem Himmel wieder mich ergetze!

Letze dich, verzagtes Herz!
Ach! Hoffnung!
Hoffnung gießt
In Sturmnacht Morgenröte!

Dieser Boden
Ist nicht Fels, nicht Moos mehr;
Diese Berge
Nicht voll schwarzen Grauses!
Ach, hier find ich wieder eine Blume!
Dieses welke Blatt,
Es lebt noch,
Harrt noch,
Daß ich seiner mich erfreue!

Seltsam! seltsam!
Find ich diese Frucht hier?
Die mir in den Gärten droben,
Ach! so lieb war –
(*Sie bricht den Granatapfel ab.*)
Laß dich genießen,
Freundliche Frucht!
Laß mich vergessen
Alle den Harm!
Wieder mich wähnen
Droben in Jugend,
In der vertaumelten
Lieblichen Zeit,
In den umduftenden
Himmlischen Blüten,

Lit up with fire,
But here, here!

Guide her here,
That I may ride up with her
Out of this dungeon!

That Phoebus may bring me
His lovely rays once more,
That Luna may
Smile at me again from her silvery tresses!

O, you hear me,
Dear father and friend,
And will raise me up
Again, again:
So that freed from long and dire torment,
I may take delight in your heaven.

Be refreshed, despondent heart!
Oh! Hope!
Hope pours the sunrise
Into the stormy night!

This ground is not rock,
No longer moss,
These mountains
Are not full of black horror!
Oh! Here I find a flower again!
This withered leaf,
It lives still,
Still firm,
That I may rejoice in it!

Strange! strange!
Do I find this fruit here
That, alas, was so dear to me
In the gardens above -
(*She breaks open the pomegranate.*)
Let me savour you,
Friendly fruit!
Let me forget
All my sorrow!
Let me pretend I am above
In my youth again
The whirl of
Those lovely days,
Amid the fragrant
Heavenly flowers,

In den Gerüchen
Seliger Wonne,
Die der Entzückten,
Der Schmachtenden ward!
(*Sie ißt einige Körner.*)
Labend! Labend!

Wie greift's auf einmal
Durch diese Freuden,
Durch diese offne Wonne
Mit entsetzlichen Schmerzen,
Mit eisernen Händen
Der Hölle durch. –
Was hab ich verbrochen,
Daß ich genoß?

Ach! Warum schafft
Die erste Freude hier mir Qual?
Was ist's? was ist's? – ihr Felsen
Scheint hier schröcklicher herabzuwinken,
Mich fester zu umfassen!
Ihr Wolken tiefer mich zu drücken!
Im fernen Schoße des Abgrunds
Dumpfe Gewitter tosend sich zu erzeugen!
Und ihr weiten Reiche der Parzen
Mir zuzurufen:
Du bist unser!

DIE PARZEN (*unsichtbar*): Du bist unser!
Ist der Ratschluß deines Ahnherrn:
Nüchtern solltest wiederkehren;
Und der Biß des Apfels macht dich unser!
Königin, wir ehren dich!

PROSERPINA: Hast du's gesprochen, Vater!
Warum? warum?
Was tat ich, daß du mich verstößest?
Warum rufst du mich nicht
Zu deinem lichten Thron auf?
Warum den Apfel?
O verflucht die Früchte!
Warum sind Früchte schön,
Wenn sie verdammen?

DIE PARZEN: Bist nun unser!
Warum trauerst du?
Sieh, wir ehren dich!
Unsre Königin!

Amid the fragrances
Of joyful bliss
That I, ravished and languished,
Once knew!
(*She eats some seeds.*)
Refreshing! Refreshing! -

But how is it
That abysmal pains
And the iron hands of Hell
Penetrate all at once
Through these joys,
Through this open bliss! –
What crime have I committed
By enjoying?

Alas! Why does this first joy
Bring me torment here?
What is it? What is it? You cliffs
Seem to glower at me more horribly,
To grip me more tightly! You clouds seem
To oppress me further!
In the depths of the abyss,
Muted thunderstorms begin to roll!
And you vast regions of the Fates
Seem to call to me:
You are ours!

THE FATES (*invisible*): You are ours!
Your ancestor has so ordained!
You were to return, sober, and the bite
of the pomegranate makes you ours!
Queen, we pay homage to you!

PROSERPINA: You have spoken, father!
Why? Why?
What did I do for you to cast me out?
Why do you not call me up
To your radiant throne?
Why the pomegranate?
O curse the fruits!
Why are fruits so beautiful
If they bring damnation?

THE FATES: Now you are ours!
Why do you lament?
See, we honor you!
Our queen!

PROSERPINA:
O wäre der Tartarus nicht eure Wohnung,
Daß ich euch hin verwünschten könnte!
O wäre der Cocyt nicht euer ewig Bad,
Daß ich für euch
Noch Flammen übrig hätte!
Ich, Königin,
Und kann euch nicht vernichten!
In ewigem Haß sei ich mit euch verbunden! –
So schöpfet, Danaiden!
Spinnt, Parzen! wütet, Furien!
In ewig gleich elendem Schicksal!
Ich beherrsche euch
Und bin darum elender als ihr alle

DIE PARZEN: Du bist unser!
Wir neigen uns dir!
Bist unser! unser!
Hohe Königin!

PROSERPINA: Fern! weg von mir
Sei eure Treu und Herrlichkeit!
Wie haß ich euch!
Und dich, wie zehnfach haß ich dich –
Weh mir! Ich fühle schon
Die verhaßten Umarmungen!

DIE PARZEN: Unser! Unsre Königin!

PROSERPINA:
Warum reckst du sie nach mir?
Recke sie nach dem Avernus!
Rufe die Qualen aus stygischen Nächten empor!
Sie steigen deinem Wink entgegen,
Nicht meine Liebe.
Wie haß ich dich
Abscheu und Gemahl,
O Pluto! Pluto!
Gib mir das Schicksal deiner Verdammten!
Nenn es nicht Liebe!
Wirf mich mit diesen Armen
In die zerstörende Qual!

DIE PARZEN: Unser! Unser! hohe Königin!

PROSERPINA:
O if only Tartarus were not already your
Dwelling that I could banish you there!
O if only Cocytus were not already
your eternal bath so that I might have
flames left over for you!
I am the queen
And I cannot annihilate you!
May I be bound to you in eternal hatred!
So draw water, Danaids!
Spin, Fates! Rage, Furies!
In an eternally wretched fate!
I govern you
And so am more wretched than you all.

FATES: You are ours!
We bow before you!
You are ours! Ours!
High queen!

PROSERPINA: Away, away from me
with your fidelity and your glory!
How I hate you'
And you, how I hate you tenfold –
Woe is me! I already feel
The abhorrent embraces.

FATES: Ours! Our queen!

PROSERPINA:
Why do you stretch out your arms to me?
Stretch them out to Avernus! Summon up
the torments up from Stygian nights!
They rise up at your bidding,
Not my love.
How I hate you
Horror and husband
O Pluto! Pluto!
Give me the fate of your damned!
Do not call it love!
Throw me with these arms
Into the destructive torment!

FATES: Ours! Our queen!

Appendix 2

Dante Gabriel Rossetti (1828-1882) *Proserpina* (1874)

Dante Gabriel Rossetti's haunting depiction of Proserpina is both beautiful and symbolic. In Rossetti's painting Proserpina is represented holding a pomegranate, which has been partially consumed. Of the painting Rossetti wrote:

> [Proserpina] is represented in a gloomy corridor of her palace, with the fatal fruit in her hand. As she passes, a gleam strikes on the wall behind her from some inlet suddenly opened, and admitting for a moment the sight of the upper world; and she glances furtively towards it, immersed in thought. The incense-burner stands beside her as an attribute of a goddess. The ivy branch in the background may be taken as a symbol of clinging memory.

The model for Rosetti's compelling image was Jane Morris, wife of Rossetti's friend and fellow artist, William Morris. Of all Rossetti's depictions of Jane Morris, Proserpina perhaps most strongly coveys Rossetti's obsession with her archetypal 'Pre-Raphaelite' looks; the rich, raven hair suggests female sexuality and yet at the same time the portrait captures his ideals of spiritual love nurtured by his constant reading of Dante. Rossetti's obsession with 'Proserpina' inspired four versions of the same image: the primary version dated 1877 (Paul Getty Jnr); a second dated 1874 (Tate Gallery); a full-scale version in coloured chalks on paper inscribed 'Proserpina' (47 x 22 inches, 119.5 x 56 cm) signed and dated 1880 and the final oil painting of 1882 (Birmingham Museum Art Gallery).

Unable to decide as a young man whether to concentrate on painting or poetry, Rossetti's work is infused with his poetic imagination and an individual interpretation of literary sources. Rossetti's accompanying sonnet to this work, 'Proserpina', written in Italian on the reverse side of the artist's full-scale image in coloured chalks, in one of Rossetti's most puzzling poems. A Petrarchan sonnet with a strict rhyme scheme, it is a poem of longing, carrying an inescapable allusion to his desire to seduce Jane from her unhappy marriage to William Morris. Although it is based on the Proserpina myth, there are clear differences. Like Goethe, Rossetti imbues Proserpina with a melancholy that reveals her inner conflict, her longing for her mother's world, despite her acknowledgement that Hades is where she belongs:

Proserpina

Afar away the light that brings cold cheer
Unto this wall, -one instant and no more
Admitted at my distant palace-door
Afar the flowers of Enna from this drear
Dire fruit, which, tasted once, must thrall me here.
Afar those skies from this Tartarean grey
That chills me and afar how far away,
The nights that shall become the days that were.

Afar from mine own self I seem, and wing
Strange ways in thought, and listen for a sign:
And still some heart unto some soul doth pine,
O whose sounds mine inner sense in fain to bring
Continually together murmuring –
'Woe me for thee, unhappy Proserpine'
Dante Gabriel Rossetti (1880)